DIRECTIONS FOR THE DECADE

LIBRARY ORIENTATION SERIES

Number one: LIBRARY ORIENTATION; Papers Presented at the First Annual Conference on Library Orientation held at Eastern Michigan University, May 7, 1971.

Number two: A CHALLENGE FOR ACADEMIC LIBRARIES: HOW TO MOTIVATE STUDENTS TO USE THE LIBRARY; Papers Presented at the Second Annual Conference on Library Orientation for Academic Libraries, Eastern Michigan University, May 4-5, 1972.

Number three: PLANNING AND DEVELOPING A LIBRARY ORIENTATION PROGRAM; Proceedings of the Third Annual Conference on Library Orientation for Academic Libraries, Eastern Michigan University, May 3-4, 1973.

Number four: EVALUATING LIBRARY USE INSTRUCTION; Papers Presented at the University of Denver Conference on the Evaluation of Library Use Instruction, December 13-14, 1973.

Number five: ACADEMIC LIBRARY INSTRUCTION: OBJECTIVES, PROGRAMS, AND FACULTY INVOLVEMENT; Papers of the Fourth Annual Conference on Library Orientation for Academic Libraries, Eastern Michigan University, May 9-11, 1974.

Number six: FACULTY INVOLVEMENT IN LIBRARY INSTRUCTION: THEIR VIEWS ON PARTICIPATION IN AND SUPPORT OF ACA—DEMIC LIBRARY USE INSTRUCTION; Papers and Summaries from the Fifth Annual Conference on Library Orientation for Academic Libraries held at Eastern Michigan University, May 15-17, 1975.

Number seven: LIBRARY INSTRUCTION IN THE SEVENTIES: STATE OF THE ART; Papers Presented at the Sixth Annual Conference on Library Orientation for Academic Libraries held at Eastern Michigan University, May 13-14, 1976.

Number eight: PUTTING LIBRARY INSTRUCTION IN ITS PLACE: IN THE LIBRARY AND IN THE LIBRARY SCHOOL; Papers Presented at the Seventh Annual Conference on Library Orientation for Academic Libraries held at Eastern Michigan University, May 12-13, 1977.

Number nine: IMPROVING LIBRARY INSTRUCTION: HOW TO TEACH AND HOW TO EVALUATE; Papers Presented at the Eighth Annual Conference on Library Orientation for Academic Libraries held at Eastern Michigan University, May 4-5, 1978.

Number ten: REFORM AND RENEWAL IN HIGHER EDUCATION: IMPLICATIONS FOR LIBRARY INSTRUCTION; Papers Presented at the Ninth Annual Conference on Library Orientation for Academic Libraries held at Eastern Michigan University, May 3-4, 1979.

Number eleven: LIBRARY INSTRUCTION AND FACULTY DEVELOPMENT: GROWTH OPPORTUNITIES IN THE ACADEMIC COMMUNITY; Papers Presented at the Twenty-Third Midwest Academic Librarians' Conference held at Ball State University, May 1978.

Number twelve: DIRECTIONS FOR THE DECADE: LIBRARY INSTRUCTION IN THE 1980s; Papers presented at the Tenth Annual Conference on Library Orientation for Academic Libraries held at Eastern Michigan University, May 8-9, 1980.

DIRECTIONS FOR THE DECADE:
LIBRARY INSTRUCTION IN THE 1980s

Papers Presented at the Tenth Annual Conference
on Library Orientation for Academic Libraries
held at Eastern Michigan University, May 8-9, 1980

edited by
Carolyn A. Kirkendall
Director, Project LOEX
Center of Educational Resources
Eastern Michigan University

Published for the
Center of Educational Resources,
Eastern Michigan University
by

Pierian Press
ANN ARBOR, MICHIGAN
1981

Library of Congress Catalog Card No. 81-80191
ISBN 0-87650-131-5

Z
711.2
L47x
no.12

Copyright © 1981, The Pierian Press
All Rights Reserved

PIERIAN PRESS
P.O. Box 1808
Ann Arbor, Michigan 48106

Contents

Preface .... page vii
    Carolyn A. Kirkendall

Assessing Library Instruction: An Author's Opinion ...... page 1
    John Lubans, Jr.

Bibliographic Instruction: An Emerging Professional
    Discipline .... page 13
    Frances L. Hopkins

Politics and Personalities ... A Panel:
    The Challenge of the 80s .... page 25
        Judith Avery
    Tuesday Morning Live — Personality and Bibliographic
    Instruction .... page 28
        Roger W. Fromm
    A Librarian for All Seasons .... page 31
        Bonnie J. King
    Personality to Education: A Necessary Change .... page 34
        Cerise Oberman-Soroka
    Why Are Most Instruction Librarians Young? .... page 36
        Virginia Tiefel

Bibliographic Instruction in the 1980s and Beyond .... page 41
    Michael Keresztesi

Post-Prandial Reactions ... A Panel:
    The Library Administrator's Role in Library
    Instruction .... page 51
        Suzanne Aiardo
    Instruction Librarians: Barriers to Information? ...... page 54
        Donald J. Kenney
    Is Knowledge of the Details of Conducting Research
    Necessary for Students Today? .... page 56
        Marilyn Lutzker
    Will This Innovation, Library Instruction, Be Adopted,
    By and By? .... page 59
        Wayne Meyer
    There Is No Real Need for Students to Know How to Use
    The Library .... page 65
        Roger Sween

User Education Evaluation .... page 71
    Nancy Fjällbrant

Library Sign Systems: An Instructional Medium .... page 91
    John Kupersmith

**Computer-Assisted Instruction in Libraries: Past, Present
and Future** .... page 99
    Mary Huston-Miyamoto

**Library Orientation and Instruction - 1979; An Annotated
Review of the Literature** .... page 119
    Hannelore B. Rader

List of Conference Participants .... page 151

Preface

Carolyn A. Kirkendall
Director
LOEX Clearinghouse

The Tenth Annual Conference on Library Orientation for Academic Libraries was held May 8 & 9, 1980, at Eastern Michigan University.

The meeting was labelled *Directions for the Decade: Library Instruction for the 1980s,* reflecting and celebrating the route of academic library instruction since its latest and greatest resurgence some ten years ago, and addressing issues of interest for the next decade.

As in recent past conferences, the theoretical approach was emphasized when possible through a series of significant presentations. Speeches covered such topics as computer-assisted instruction, library sign systems as part of the instruction program, an analytical approach to bibliographic instruction for the advanced researcher, library user education evaluation, and the perceptions of instruction librarians of their own role and professional mission. A personal summary of the present state of academic library instruction started the meeting, and included suggestions for what is and will be required for adequate present and future provision of this particular library service so zealously supported by its promoters.

Readers of these proceedings are requested to keep three points in mind: for the sake of unity, and although the conference itself addresses a broad range of user education topics, the term "orientation" was kept in the meeting title; spoken presentations do not always result in consistently readable copy; this publication contains speeches in the order in which they were presented.

An annotated bibliography of related literature published during 1979 is appended, as is a listing of all conference participants and speakers.

In addition to the formal presentations which have always comprised the main body of our conference programs, two informal panels were also scheduled. A "call for opinion-statement papers" was issued and ten respondents were selected. In this case, it was hoped that some of the personal concerns and problems inherent and encountered in library instruction work could be briefly and candidly shared with the audience. It was not the scholarly and documented presentations which were requested for these panel formats, but some original and lively reaction to these kinds of intriguing questions:

---why do most instruction librarians seem to be young?
---is library instruction a duty generally considered appropriate for the beginning librarian?
---does the success of an orientation/instruction project depend 90% on the personality of the individual librarian?
---why don't job descriptions for library directors include the requirement "must be committed to library instruction?"
---what are the limitations of instruction? Where won't it work? Is it always necessary to provide it?
---if instruction is successful, and more and more faculty want their students to receive it, will a good working program become a monster, and create more and more work?

As the state-of-the-art of academic library instruction at conference time had been or was to be concurrently summarized in three separate published articles by the LOEX Clearinghouse Director,[1] the usual annual LOEX review of the national scene was not presented during the conference program itself, but distributed in bits via the LOEX newsletters and via a statistical summary sheet provided to each conference attendant. These figures are also included in an appendix to this preface.

Small group discussions again provided the opportunity to informally react to topics and issues addressed during the conference, and allowed participants to share their own opinions with others working in similar academic environments. Appreciation is extended to those who willingly participated as group discussion leaders.

Participants were hosted to a wine party and a cocktail party sponsored respectively by Neal-Schuman Publishers of New York and by the Pierian Press of Ann Arbor, Michigan. These annual

---

1. The articles are: Kirkendall, Carolyn A. "Cooperation, coordination and communication: the LOEX experience," *Library User Education: Are New Approaches Needed?* Proceedings of the 1979 Cambridge First International Conference on User Education, London: British Library, 1980; "Information exchanges for library instruction: committees, clearinghouses and concerns," *Drexel Library Quarterly*, to be published; and "Library use education: current practices and trends," *Library Trends* 29:1, Summer 1980, p. 29–37.

occasions provide a welcome setting for both socializing and informally exchanging information, and the LOEX Clearinghouse continues to greatly appreciate the support and generosity of these sponsors.

Special recognition is also extended to all speakers for their thought-provoking remarks, to the staff of McKenny Union for its consistently excellent support service, to Hannelore Rader for preparing the annual bibliography, most gratefully to the LOEX Secretary Kathy Graham, to the printing and photography services at EMU, and particularly to Paul Borawski, under whose capable and cooperative direction the EMU Division of Continuing Education's non-credit program functions and provides a unit of continuing education credit for all conference participants.

ACADEMIC LIBRARY INSTRUCTION STATISTICS
Prepared by the LOEX Clearinghouse -- May 1980

	December 1979 (base of 830)		May 1973 (base of 193)	
ENROLLMENT LEVELS				
Under 1,000	23 percent*	(194)		
1,000–4,999	37 percent	(305)		
5,000–9,999	17 percent	(144)		
10,000–14,999	8 percent	(70)		
15,000–20,000	8 percent	(64)		
20,000+	6 percent	(53)		
TYPE OF LIBRARY				
Community/Technical/Two–Year	25 percent	(209)	22 percent	(31)
Undergraduate	14 percent	(119)	21 percent	(29)
Graduate	3 percent	(26)	7 percent	(9)
Undergraduate/Graduate	48 percent	(395)	46 percent	(64)
Divisional	7 percent	(55)	4 percent	(6)
Special	3 percent	(26)		
STAFFING/PERSONNEL				
Part–Time Duty	91 percent	(759)	91 percent	(126)
Full–Time Duty	9 percent	(71)	2 percent	(3)

	December 1979 (base of 830)		May 1973 (base of 193)	
PROGRAM ADMINISTRATION				
Through Reference Department	35 percent	(287)		
Separate Division/Coordinator	4 percent	(37)		
Haphazard/No Response	70 percent			
LIBRARY INSTRUCTION MANDATORY	24 percent	(200)		
LEVELS PROVIDED INSTRUCTION				
Freshman	79 percent	(656)		
Sophomore	56 percent	(465)		
Junior	45 percent	(370)		
Senior	44 percent	(369)		
Transfer	28 percent	(229)		
Faculty	31 percent	(254)	35 percent	(49)
Special	51 percent	(420)		
INSTRUCTIONAL METHODS				
Credit Courses	42 percent	(347)	22 percent	(30)
Seminars/Workshops	33 percent	(274)		
Term Paper Clinics	21 percent	(173)		
Lectures	95 percent	(790)	73 percent	(102)
Computer-Assisted	2 percent	(18)	4 percent	(6)
Point-of-Use Programs	69 percent	(575)		
Tours: Conducted	81 percent	(670)	76 percent	(105)
Tours: Tape	10 percent	(87)	11 percent	(15)

	December 1979 (base of 830)		May 1973 (base of 193)	
Instructional methods continued				
Tours: Slide/Tape	17 percent	(139)	9 percent	(12)
Tours: Printed Self-Guided	32 percent	(263)	19 percent	(26)
Individualized Instruction	67 percent	(558)	62 percent	(86)
INSTRUCTIONAL MATERIALS				
PRINT:				
Bibliographies	56 percent	(468)	65 percent	(90)
Study Guides/Pathfinders	40 percent	(335)	37 percent	(51)
Guides to Tools	49 percent	(405)		
Exercises	38 percent	(318)	35 percent	(49)
Workbooks	11 percent	(90)	14 percent	(19)
Library Handbooks/Guides--Student	55 percent	(456)	60 percent	(84)
Library Handbooks/Guides--Faculty	22 percent	(179)	23 percent	(32)
Miscellaneous Handouts	44 percent	(363)		
NON-PRINT:				
Transparencies	40 percent	(330)	15 percent	(21)
Slides	17 percent	(145)	20 percent	(27)
Slide/Tapes	37 percent	(306)	34 percent	(47)
Tape/Cassettes	25 percent	(204)	24 percent	(24)
Video	13 percent	(105)	11 percent	(15)
Film	6 percent	(53)	6 percent	(8)
Filmstrips	13 percent	(106)	11 percent	(15)
None Used	28 percent	(236)	23 percent	(32)

	December 1979 (base of 830)	May 1973 (base of 193)
EVALUATION METHODS		
None Used	52 percent (414)	30 percent (42)
Informal (Faculty)	7 percent (58)	14 percent (20)
Informal (Student)	5 percent (45)	12 percent (16)
Informal (Library Staff)	1 percent (10)	5 percent (7)
Testing	7 percent (59)	17 percent (24)
Written Feedback (Student)	20 percent (164)	22 percent (31)
Written Feedback (Faculty)	9 percent (74)	
Validated Control Groups	1 percent (11)	1 percent (2)
Faculty Committee Review	.07 percent (6)	
General Impressions of Student Performance	2 percent (18)	
PUBLICITY METHODS		
Signs/Posters	26 percent (216)	9 percent (13)
Personal Faculty Contact	79 percent (657)	80 percent (112)
Letters to Faculty	35 percent (289)	9 percent (12)
Student Newspaper Announcements	31 percent (257)	41 percent (57)
Faculty Newsletter Announcements	20 percent (168)	
Faculty Committee Announcements	10 percent (79)	
ENGAGED IN ORIENTATION/INSTRUCTION RESEARCH	39 percent (324)	14 percent (27)

*All percentages are rounded off.

ASSESSING LIBRARY INSTRUCTION:
AN AUTHOR'S OPINION

John Lubans, Jr.
University of Houston–
Downtown Campus

It is a pleasure to be here at this tenth LOEX meeting. We've come a long way since the first meeting and we do have a lot to celebrate.

Our umbrella theme, "directions for the decade," suggests I do some crystal ball gazing and maybe even get out on some tree limbs. How many of you have heard of Eddie Chiles? For those of you who have not, he is a Texas industrial incensed about governmental interference. This concerns him so much he's bought up TV time for spot announcements that usually start with his statement of "I'm mad." If you want, you can write in and get a red bumper sticker from Eddie which proclaims in bold letters "I'm mad too, Eddie!" For a while since I am to do a critical overview I thought that bumper sticker might serve as a good title for what may sound like so much grouching about. Perhaps it can serve as a subtitle. Keeping that in mind my talk will attempt to survey where we've been, what some recent trends suggest, and what we've yet to do. Throughout this conference, I look forward to hearing about what other people think about where the library instruction movement may be headed.

Celebration

I said we have a lot to celebrate. Library use instruction programs and practitioners have proliferated during the decade. True progress can be seen in organizational developments in the state and national associations and in many conference programs when they address library use instruction in all types of libraries. A mixing of librarians and ideas is just now beginning to be accepted as routine.[1] We appear to be finally recognizing that we share the same user. It bears repeating: we share the same user. After all, the college freshman that stumbles or is propelled into the college library, has been to other libraries. Even more surprising for some of us may be the fact that this same student has already endured more instruction on information finding and use than we'd advocate giving in the entire freshman year. Anne Hyland has a convincing demonstration of this. She's pinned up behind her desk the library curriculum skills chart from the Calgary Board of Education: a 3 x 4 *foot* matrix of over 180 skills.[2] Teachers, when they casually suggest a quick lesson on the library are, to say the least, impressed by the coverage when Anne queries them about *which* of the 180 skills they'd like covered.

Several public libraries, in only the last two years or so, are programming for educating the library user. The Berkeley-Oakland study now underway should be an eye opener for many other public librarians.[3]

In England, research agencies have moved beyond haphazard or token support of the concept of educating the library user. Research is being conducted in all types of libraries and has the attention of the National Book League which would be equivalent to our gaining the support of the Center for the Book at the Library of Congress if we were so fortunate. Over this past Christmas I visited Loughborough University and shared in a seminar with Ann Irving, Mike Brittain and a dozen or so other librarians from public, school and academic library settings several hours of discussion on our common problems. From the give and take of this group I would surmise they are more advanced on the cooperative road than we. They are more aware of sharing the same user than we seem to be.

The most obvious growth and development is closest to us in academic libraries. Carolyn Kirkendall was kind enough to share with me her manuscript on library use education which will be published in the summer issue of *Library Trends*. I've found her survey data to be quite indicative of instruction activities during much of the last decade. Table 1 compares the responses to two surveys done by LOEX; one in 1973 and the other in 1979.

Means of teaching are broken into print and non-print. The former includes bibliographies, exercises, handbooks and the latter encompasses film in all its varieties. The increases over the years which most of us have believed were occurring are confirmed by the survey. The mean numbers of both print and non-print productions have just about doubled. The combined means add up to 4.65 in 1979 which is a sizeable increase over the combined total of 2.5 in 1973.

This growth is carried even further in the analysis of the types of programs (e.g., lectures, tours, individualized and computer assisted instruction). Under the category of programs in Table 1, one sees that double the effort and activity is now expended by the reporting libraries. In 1973 one could find about two programs while in 1979 well over four programs are put on by each of the 830 responding libraries. Librarians are indeed "bullish" about library use instruction.

TABLE 1

INSTRUCTION ACTIVITIES	RESPONSES 1979 (830)	RESPONSES 1973 (193)
MEANS OF TEACHING:		
PRINT	2614 Mean=3.15	325 Mean=1.68
NON--PRINT	1249 Mean=1.5	157 Mean= .81
PROGRAMS	3894 Mean=4.69	382 Mean=1.98
EVALUATION?		
YES:	445 Mean= .54*	100 Mean= .52*
NO:	414 Mean= .52	42(+51n.r.) Mean= .48

*Based on each year's total respondents.

Source: From tables in Carolyn Kirkendall, "Library Use Education: Current Practices and Trends," *Library Trends*, Summer, 1980 (in press).

Sobering Up

A less encouraging trend in Table 1 is seen in librarians finding out how effective their educational efforts are. Evaluation appears to have made little progress, at least if we only look at the numbers. The means for each year, if we spread out all the evaluation efforts over all the respondents, are about the same; .54 in 1979 and .52 in 1973. One might try to explain this away on the basis that only some programs on a campus are evaluated while others are not. But this does not hold since one half stated in 1979 they did no evaluation. *None*. Now while this may be all right since some programs need little evaluation, it is disconcerting to see the types of evaluations being done. Written feedback by students is the most frequent technique, with faculty feedback a distant second; testing, third; and "informal" evaluation with faculty, fourth. Only one percent or a total of 11 libraries report using "validated control groups" which may include some substantive evaluatory work.

Let's leave evaluation for the moment and briefly look at some other unresolved aspects: *redundancy*, the *remedial aspect, lack of acceptance by non-librarians*, and how the *grass roots nature* of our programs relate to these problems.

Redundancy. For quick proof, examine some curriculum plans put out by state education agencies. The repetitive nature of user education becomes obvious. Must the *Readers' Guide* be emphasized in the fourth, sixth and ninth grades? Apparently, since we rarely fail to emphasize it again at the freshman year. As an example, let us look at the recent commercial filmstrip featuring the stoneage cartoon characters Bamm--Bamm and Pebbles.[4] It is used in junior and senior high school but covers the same issues to be found in many library instruction programs at the college level. The filmstrip starts off conventionally enough. Teenage Bamm--Bamm needs help in using the library and his friend, Pebbles, enthusaistically attempts to instruct him about the mysteries of the Reference Room. The two are soon discussing a wide span of reference tools, from *Who's Who of American Women*, and *Current Biography*, to an advanced introduction to *Moody's* (corporate manuals!) and periodical indexing format. Bamm--Bamm, one assumes, leaves the Reference Room up to handling any prehistoric information problems he may encounter.

Closely allied with redundancy (about which *we* can do something if nothing more than sharing our productions) is the *remedial* nature of much of the work we do. The fault for this lies at some one-else's door. While Bamm--Bamm learns all about the library in the ninth and eleventh grades he will have forgotten all he has learned by his freshman year or year of entry into the job market. It is believed that one learns best by doing, doing, and doing, again. While we would like to imagine that library skills instruction is as a continuous thread throughout one's education it is not the case. The education establishment at best pays lip service to the concept of information use. As a result assignments stressing information use are all too infrequent and we keep starting from scratch vainly searching for the thread. It happens at the university, too.[5]

It is implied above that there is a *lack of acceptance* by Education of some of our ideas (I include both educators and students). If we ask someone if they think knowing how to find and use information is good, they will of course respond in the affirmative. If we ask a faculty if the library is the heart of the university, to a person they will assent. Now ask people if they agree with this statement "Most people know very little about finding and using information."

This is somewhat akin to saying most people have a low information IQ. Unless you are dealing with a submissive audience the response will be polite; they will agree to a small extent and invariably exempt themselves from this affliction from which a few others may suffer. Convincing someone that they have a need to improve their "information IQ" when they don't perceive they have to is not an easy undertaking as many of us have discovered. Jon Lindgren, writing in *Progress in Educating the Library User*, says it best: "Students, faculty, and administrators embrace a myth . . . that grievously wants exploding; that libraries are easy to use."[6] In user studies I've done, many of the respondents express confidence in doing library research term papers. Of course they know what a thesis statement is! An example they supply is: "The Mafia in the U.S.," and they know how to find the latest and most relevant information on the topic: it's in a year-old issue of the *Readers' Digest*!

Perhaps we need to borrow from others' experience in alerting people to unknown needs. Madison Avenue must have faced it in making certain commercials for television. Imagine this scenario:

A crowded classroom of students. The instructor is returning term papers. It is the end of the Spring term; a very warm day. The camera pans over the looks of dismay on their perspiring faces as the students see their grades. One bursts into tears. Finally, it stops at a smiling face, obviously one of the few A papers. The voice-over intones: "Aren't you glad you used *P.A.I.S.*?"

If this doesn't appeal, a less mass media approach might. We could insert labels into library books referring one, in times of an information anxiety attack, to the "bibliographic instruction clinic." This approach was tried by some public libraries for their problem patrons for psychiatric referrals, but was ruled ethically akin to painting diapers on nude children in picture books.

One could go on but I will spare you.

The difficulty of gaining acceptance is due in part to the *grass roots level* of our concerns. Organizationally library use instruction is unique. Its recent development has been with little if any support from administrators. While library directors and other library managers have mastered the warehousing aspects of libraries and some of the retailing functions, e.g., displaying and labeling and making available, they have yet to emphasize the selling and buying function or marketing to the consumer. We are just now entering an era where "service to users" may actually mean something. The major reason in this recent twist is economic. Hard nosed accountability and fierce budgetary competition have required the library to do something. It can no longer afford the luxury of relying on its being a sacred "public good." Perhaps with the control now gained over library facilities and resources more of the decision makers will see the relationship of library use to funding support. It is interesting to muse over Michael Gorman's recent essay on famous catalogers like Panizzi, Lubetzky, and Bliss which concludes that the one feature of their lives and works is the belief that "libraries exist to serve their users."[7] As administrators pay more attention to operationalizing a concept such as Ranganathan's "right book to the right user at the right time," the grass roots commitment may be augmented by administrative support within the library and, more importantly, the administrators may take it outside the library. Our potential in gaining educational change rises sharply if this were to happen. Consider the potential impact of the user education movement if "access," now a meaningless buzz word, had been defined and clarified at the White House Conference as much as the National Periodicals Center has been recently discussed in Washington by library directors and political leaders.

Moving Beyond

My partial solution is not novel; it is one among many others; it is prosaic. If competence in library use is to be embraced and acted upon by people outside of librarianship then conclusive evidence of benefits needs to be marshalled forth. Earlier, in Table 1, we examined LOEX survey data, and found that while evaluation is practiced in several different ways there has been little change in the quantity or quality in the evaluation of our efforts from 1973 to 1979. It bears repeating that in fact one-half of the reporting libraries do not evaluate. One assumes they either deduce the reasons for their success or failure normatively or have no fixed idea of what their program is meant to achieve. While the methods of evaluation we do employ may verify the merits of individual programs none seems geared, even collectively, to demonstrating the overall value of one's gaining information finding and using skills. While some programs of instruction may be well established, have campus-wide support and enjoy large numbers of participants, and therefore may not need assessment (at least not solely for proving merit), most of our programs could benefit from well-conducted evaluation. One should also bear in mind the benefits *other* libraries may gain from seeing what worked or didn't work at another library. For that matter, even those programs that are now judged "outstanding" one might question if this is because of the program or because of the elite nature of the participants. Let me clarify. I've always been impressed with the University of California at Berkeley Bibliography 100 credit course and its repeated ability to attract hundreds of students. Internally the program is not that different from many others – in fact many may have been modeled after it. Yet the success that Berkeley has had for a credit course is not to my knowledge matched on any other campuses. Why? For that matter, do we know what influence the instruction program has on a student's ability at Berkeley or at other campuses with similar programs?

We have yet to show a casual link between user education and improved levels of information finding and use.

When we do not measure our impact and yet make claims about the effects, the research design looks like Diagram A in Table 2 (borrowing notation from the social science wherein the "0" indicates an observation at a certain point in time and an "X" represents a "treatment" at a specific time. "R" stands for statistical randomness of selection of participants.)[8]

If, after a film loop on short story explicators has been installed at a point of need, we can only make evaluatory comments such as, "We think we get fewer questions on short stories," then we have missed out on an opportunity to statistically measure the instructional value of this film loop and perhaps convince administrators for further support. Without knowing where we were before the program, (*viz.*, the number of questions) we can hardly say with certainty where we are now (*viz.*, that fewer questions are asked). With supporting data, what may be regarded trivially and referred to as a "toy" in reference can become an important and necessary "tool" of library business.

Diagram B shows perhaps the commonest approach, written feedback and quizzes. A better design might be to add a before to the after measure, or a pretest/posttest in order to say how great an effect has been felt: Diagram C.[9] This would help arrive at a more meaningful result. By adding a control group (Diagram D) we further improve the statements we can make about the value of our instruction especially when statistically contrasting the benefits gained from taking part in a program. I have a pet research design which would work well to test the benefits of workbooks and library instruction on term papers versus traditional catch-as-catch-can faculty-sponsored library instruction. It is illustrated in Diagram E.

This approach to an experiment takes into account most of the criticisms that would be levied against evaluation of any program. It is sophisticated and expensive but would serve to convincingly demonstrate the effect of a program.

One evaluation done at the University of Colorado, while weakened because of some external, unexpected factors, did produce some usable results. I include them here because the differences in the response are statistically significant. It makes use of a control group of students. The evaluation consists of a questionnaire sent to two groups, the two program groups in Economics and History

TABLE 2

EVALUATION DESIGNS

DIAGRAM A		X	

DIAGRAM B		X O	POST INSTRUCTION ANALYSIS

DIAGRAM C		0 X 0	PRE AND POST INSTRUCTION OBSERVATION

DIAGRAM D		0 X 0 0 0	CONTROL GROUP

DIAGRAM E	R
	R
	R
	R
		0_1 X 0_2
		0_3 0_4
		         X 0_5
		               0_6
			"SOLOMON"

DIAGRAM F		0 0 X 0 0	TIME SERIES

and the control group of a sample of University of Colorado students.[10] While imperfect, the evaluation results are encouraging as can be seen in Table 3. The response by the student participants was significantly different from that of the random sample. It presents a positive impact as an outcome of the program. To augment the evaluation of students the faculty were surveyed concurrently and their opinions are represented on the bottom half of Table 3.

TABLE 3

PROGRAM IMPACT ON STUDENTS

AFFIRMATIVE RESPONSE IN PERCENTAGES

	History and Economics Students		Random Sample
Asking for assistance	73	72	56
Being referred	32	24	9
Coursework helps develop library research techniques	58	47	37
Class assignments requiring library use	59	48	36

PROGRAM IMPACT ON FACULTY

	History	Economics
Now require more library use	46	50
Students now are better able to do research	64	90
Support allocation of departmental space	82	82

My point is to show that heavily quantified studies are not the only type that can give one some measure of the impact of a program. Rather, asking participants for their judgments may serve a useful purpose in what is termed "illuminative" evaluation.

Other measures could be used as well to measure program improvements. Circulation and non-circulation data are now easily kept by departmental major of borrower. Comparing such data among departments (those with library instruction programs and those without) might be enlightening. For example, in a time series over five years (Diagram F in Table 2) one might expect some differences to appear.

We need to overcome our reluctance to keep track of what we do. Other professionals have -- every minute of their time is accounted for. We need to compare data, which now is easily available, to our instructional efforts. At the most easily quantified level one should be able to answer the question of does a newly-installed sign program reduce the number of directional questions. Over a semester, following an intensive instructional effort, do the types of questions asked change?

Summing Up

Well, we have done a lot and a lot remains to be done. What will we say about our programs in 1990? Will we be able to convincingly say there is a link between user education and improved levels of information finding and use? Will we be able to demonstrate that through user education there is a strengthening of the library's role in people's lives?

NOTES

1. *RQ* of ALA's Reference and Adult Services Division will feature, as of Summer 1980, "Library Literacy," a column on library instruction in all types of libraries.

2. Anne Hyland discusses this chart on page 34 of her chapter in *Progress in Educating the Library User*, edited by John Lubans, Jr., New York: Bowker, 1978.

3. *News Release: Oakland-Berkeley Library Project*, School of Library and Information Studies, University of California, Berkeley, December 18, 1979.

4. *Bamm--Bamm in Information Please -- Unit III: More Reference Tools* (filmstrip/cassette) Hanna-Barbera Productions, Inc., Educational Division, [1979].

5. One of the most important but little recognized essays in the 1974 volume, *Educating the Library User* is Professor Robert Pois' on the lecture-textbook syndrome.

6. Jon Lindgren, "Seeking a Useful Tradition for Library User Instruction" in *Progress in Educating the Library User*, edited by John Lubans, Jr., New York: Bowker, 1978, p. 71.

7. Michael Gorman, "Towards Bibliographic Control," *American Libraries*, April 1980, p. 203.

8. Donald T. Campbell and Julian C. Stanley, *Experimental and Quasi-Experimental Design for Research*, Chicago: Rand McNally, 1963.

9. For an example of a well-done modern test, see Anne Hyland's *The Ohio School Library/Media Test*, Toledo, Ohio: Ward Artcraft Printing Company, 1978.

10. [John Lubans, Jr.] *Final Report to the Council on Library Resources and the National Endowment for the Humanities . . . Program to Improve and Increase Student and Faculty Involvement in Library Use*. Boulder, Colorado: University of Colorado, 1978.

BIBLIOGRAPHIC INSTRUCTION: AN EMERGING PROFESSIONAL DISCIPLINE

Frances L. Hopkins
Franklin & Marshall College

It is my intention in this paper to examine the forces that I think are pushing toward the differentiation of bibliographic instruction into a distinct specialty that will have more in common with an academic discipline than with traditional academic librarianship.

I am very glad, therefore, to see on the program for this afternoon a panel discussion on "Politics and Personalities" followed by a paper about a conceptual approach to bibliographic instruction. As I see it, the differentiation of bibliographic instruction from the rest of academic librarianship is the inevitable political effect of a combination of personality and conceptual factors that are operating within the bibliographic instruction movement. I have no prior knowledge about what any of the other speakers plan to say, but I hope that this paper will serve as a useful introduction -- perhaps even a framework -- for this afternoon's program.

I.

Let us examine the present state of the bibliographic movement in terms of its institutional and conceptual development.

Obviously, bibliographic instruction has made worthy institutional progress during the past decade and one-half. A high proportion of college and university libraries now offer user instruction at some level, professional associations and conferences are being sustained by a loyal membership, and most job ads for reference librarians specify instructional responsibilities. Most important, perhaps, we have had the Council on Library Resources/National Endowment for the Humanities grants to spur research and development in a variety of institutional environments. Yet this apparent success is precarious indeed. I am not thinking here about the obvious need to proselytize among the academic disciplines, but about the uncertain permanence of our impact on the individual academic libraries in which we work.

Mary Biggs, after a stint as coordinator of a grant-funded BI project, was sharply critical of the poor quality of professional work and of administrative policies that condone it. "It comes as no surprise to any capable and candid librarian," she wrote, "that a distressing number of our colleagues are skating along day by day on the edge of incompetency."[1] The problem involves, she continued, not only the expected "insecurity and antipathy of technical service librarians," but, more significantly, " . . . the need for more and better public service librarians, [including the] evaluation and development (and possibly reassignment or replacement) . . . of current staff . . . . In libraries without enthusiastic administrative support for instruction [these problems] may be insurmountable."[2]

If we find older librarians unequal to instructional responsibilities, who will replace them? At the 1977 LOEX conference, Anne Beaubien and her colleagues at the University of Michigan criticized library schools at length for their almost total failure to train budding academic librarians in either the content or techniques of library instruction.[3] I might add that, unlike most graduate and professional programs, library schools do almost nothing to socialize their students to a particular career world. Most new academic librarians seem to have very little understanding of the academic enterprise, and they are quite naive about the political problems of library instruction programs.

Nor can we place much hope in library administrators. Joe Boissé, at the time library director at the University of Wisconsin–Parkside, stated at the same LOEX conference, " . . . the majority of directors of academic libraries understand neither what bibliographic instruction really is, nor what its rightful place in the library should be."[4]

In the most telling commentary of all, Nancy Gwinn, program officer for Council on Library Resources, recently identified staff turnover and lack of administrative support as important factors in the indifferent success of the bibliographic instruction projects they have funded. In consequence, CLR has now ceased its grants for bibliographic instruction development per se and will instead work with academic libraries on "management and institutional planning, in order for instructional services to attain their rightful place among the library's priorities and goals."[5] In other words, even academic institutions that have accepted thousands of dollars from a granting agency to develop bibliographic instruction programs have not always honored their implied commitments to support those programs administratively during the grant period or to extend them with financial support beyond it.

How is it, then, that bibliographic instruction has survived and even flourished? Earlham's program, one of the oldest in continuous existence, has prospered for two obvious reasons. First, the initiating and sustaining force behind the program has been the library director himself; no one lower in the organization had to persuade him to set the necessary administrative priorities. Second, and surely related to the library's management, staff stability in key positions has allowed the smooth integration of a succession of young librarians into the ongoing instructional program. But Earlham is not the norm.

The consensus seems to be that a great many programs owe their existence to the enthusiasm and drive of individuals with a mission. In fact, personality has been an element of fundamental importance in the bibliographic instruction movement. To quote my friend Kay Rottsalk of St. Olaf College, "Most successful instruction librarians I know are confident, articulate, subject rather than technically oriented, aggressive (tenacious?), professionally committed, mature, curious, concerned with people but not necessarily extroverted, risk-takers, and bore easily."[6] About the only trait she left out is that they also tend to be workaholics.

It is fair to suspect, I would say, that any library service whose quality or survival depends in very many libraries on such a special kind of personality has not yet been accepted by the professional establishment into the normal institutional structure. The problem is that the bureaucracy of academic librarianship imposes regular clerical office hours, an incessant flow of office management tasks, and a hierarchical form of governance, and sets, unfortunately, only mediocre standards for performance.

Any hard-working, creative, achievement-oriented individual will chafe at such constraints, but where colleagues are moderately responsive and administrators reasonably flexible and supportive, he or she can in time guide a BI program to an advanced level. Where the situation is less benign, however, fatigue and frustration will inevitably set in. Ultimately, when supervision passes on to someone else -- usually to someone more amenable to bureaucratic norms -- vision is lost and the program shrinks to the dimensions of its most routine components.

Conceptually, the bibliographic instruction movement has also had mixed success. We have for some years had at our command a variety of well-designed and tested teaching models: the workbook for basic library skills, the AV presentation on the use of individual bibliographic tools, the fifty-minute lecture-demonstration on specialized subject bibliography and search strategy, and the comprehensive course for credit. But in the past year or two it has often been said that the bibliographic instruction movement has reached a plateau. There seems to be a pervasive feeling among experienced instruction librarians that something more is needed -- some kind of breakthrough. We have long since passed the stage of conceiving of library instruction as simply a means of imparting procedural skills and an awareness of resources, but we still have no clear consensus on what its mission should be.

Part of the problem, I believe, is that the technocracy dominant in academic librarianship as a whole – the value system which takes technical considerations to be ends in themselves – dictates that librarians must be content to access information and should not aspire to impart knowledge.

I do not mean to use the terms "bureaucracy" and "technocracy" with entirely pejorative connotation here. They are not forms of occupational life that I find personally congenial, but they are forms that have resulted quite legitimately from human efforts to deal efficiently with genuine problems. My point is rather that the bibliographic instruction movement, although it has emerged from a bureaucratic/technocratic system, is in fact responding to a set of problems that cannot by their nature be treated effectively within a bureaucratic and technocratic context.

II.

What is it about bibliographic instruction that makes for this poor fit? As instructional goals and techniques have become more ambitious, bibliographic instruction has become more and more demanding of librarians' time, commitment, and intellectual curiosity.

Basic library skills instruction, the simplest level, may take time and effort to prepare, but it does not force librarians to look beyond familiar tools and procedures. It can be absorbed fairly readily, therefore, as an add-on service in most reference departments.

Course-related bibliographic instruction requires a deeper involvement in teaching. It is possible to teach subject bibliography superficially, with broad descriptive annotations and purely schematic search strategy. (In fact, my first library director strongly suggested that I prepare all my handouts without leaving the reference desk, by copying entries straight out of Winchell!) But serious instruction librarians invest hours relating the idiosyncracies of various reference sources to specific student needs and working through sample topics to illustrate the most common search strategy problems in the given subject field. Moreover, preparation time is only half the story. Where librarians produce well-wrought instruction sessions, reference work gradually changes from an ad hoc, reactive sort of information service to a consultative, proactive research advisory service. It is a lot harder, in the latter situation, to leave the reference desk at an appointed hour, knowing that students still need guidance, especially when it was one's own BI session that generated their need.

Recently, interest has been turning to a third level, namely, integrated bibliographic instruction, which involves the librarian even more deeply in teaching. This trend has been encouraged by NEH and CLR, who have awarded grants mainly to programs -- again using Nancy Gwinn's words -- "based on concepts generated by Patricia Knapp's Monteith College library experiment."[7] I am sure all of you know that Patricia Knapp's work was an elaboration of her basic principle that library research competency is a genuine liberal art -- right next to writing competency as an attribute of the educated person.

Course-related bibliographic instruction typically supports a pre-existing research assignment, usually a term paper. Integrated instruction, in contrast, is incorporated into a course more as an end in itself, because students need to experience certain research processes in order to grasp certain aspects of course content.

An example that I think illustrates integrated instruction particularly well is a library assignment reported by Virginia Parr at the University of Oregon.[8] Psychology students there are given plausible journalistic statements of controversial issues which make use of popularized psychological knowledge. The students must first analyze the statements into researchable assumptions and then, using reference sources and search strategies taught previously in the classroom, must locate in the literature of psychology evidence for or against those assumptions. They then rewrite the paragraphs to reflect the current state of knowledge in the discipline, citing all their sources, of course. The exercise is designed to show new psychology majors the difference between the layperson's approach and the scholarly or clinical approach to psychological questions and evidence and to show students how important it is to read the popular press critically. At the same time, it gives them a basic working knowledge of the literature of their major field.

At this level of bibliographic instruction, the librarian becomes involved in initial course planning and plays a key role in designing and grading the library assignment. Beyond that, as students work through such an assignment, the librarian establishes a mentor relationship with them that tends to persist through subsequent courses.

Somewhere along this continuum from skills instruction to integrated bibliographic instruction there occurs an irreversible personal metamorphosis from librarian to teacher. In course-related instruction, one is still primarily librarian, serving as fifty-minute resource person in someone else's classroom, demonstrating techniques for identifying and accessing library resources. But close involvement with students in consultative follow-up reference work or in integrated instruction, observing in detail their actual behavior in a research situation, immediately reveals why the teaching of research skills and resources alone is inadequate. There is a vast gulf between knowing about the bibliographic resources in a field of study and understanding how to do a coherent piece of library research. Only by identifying and analyzing the mistakes students actually make when they try to locate information or compile a bibliography can we discover the patterns of ignorance and misunderstanding that interfere with productive library research.

How can a student do a decent literature search, for instance, without understanding the distinctions between primary and secondary sources; between documented scholarship and expressions of opinion, popular or expert, on controversial social issues; between evaluative and non-evaluative bibliographies? Students have great difficulty with such concepts until they have actually used them in several individually guided research activities.

To use standard reference sources successfully, students often need to understand such things as the reasons for the variant name forms that complicate research on historical or non-western topics and the reasons for discrepancies of fact or interpretation in reference books of different vintage or different editorial policy.

Even advanced undergraduates, one discovers, may have no notion of the nature of a scholarly discipline, the existence of different theory groups within disciplines, or the changes in approach and methodology over time that can turn a grand old reference source like the Hastings *Encyclopedia of Religion and Ethics* into more of a primary source for contemporary users. (I should not mention, perhaps, that many librarians are equally ignorant of these things.)

I could go on and on with examples, but the general problem should be apparent: in order to use library resources effectively, students need to connect them with a basic understanding of how knowledge is created, communicated, and synthesized within fields of inquiry, how knowledge differs structurally from one field to another, and how bibliographic resources reflect the various stages of the knowledge process. Faculty want to teach subject content, not structure, to undergraduates. And, in fact, they rarely have reason to examine the structures of their own disciplines in terms of bibliographic systems and patterns of scholarly activity. The instruction librarian, therefore, once he or she recognizes the need, must assume this responsibility. But there is very little in most librarians' training, work experience, or ideology that prepares them to do so.

III.

The call for a theoretical base for bibliographic instruction has by now become a discernible theme in the literature, but there is also some hesitancy to associate the notion of "theory" with a pursuit that most people think of in terms of skills and technique. A recent article by Jon Lindgren reminds us that composition teachers are also imparting skills and technique -- they are teaching, he says, a process and a craft rather than subject content -- yet they have shown that analysis of a craft can be carried to a fairly sophisticated level and can result in a coherent, teachable body of knowledge.[9] The difference that Lindgren points out is that composition teachers can draw on a long and respected tradition in the ancient study of rhetoric, while we have nothing of the sort. Lindgren, as I read him, suggests that we seek out and/or create a body of relevant knowledge that can *become* our scholarly tradition.

There does, in fact, exist a discipline which has begun to produce a respectable corpus of theory and research about the patterns of production, communication, synthesis, and use of knowledge within various fields of inquiry and about the corresponding structure of their literatures. It is quite a new discipline, scarcely recognized before the 1960s. It has been called by such various uneuphonious names as "social epistemology," "episto-dynamics," "catenics" (from the Latin word for chain), "informatics," or simply "the science of research."[10] It is an interdisciplinary mix of sociology, history, and philosophy of knowledge and quantitative studies of scholarly publication and citation patterns. So far, it has been concerned primarily with the sciences, but interest in applying the same analytic methods to social science and humanistic fields is beginning to appear.

We are still a very long way from developing a coherent, teachable body of material useful in undergraduate bibliographic instruction, but I am convinced that this relatively new discipline will provide the necessary theoretical base. Enough work has already been done to prove its relevance to bibliographic instruction in the sciences and some social sciences. In the humanities, especially in literature and other areas which are not organized as formal disciplines, it is less clear how a sociological study of scholarship can illuminate the bibliographic research process for undergraduates. Now that basic research is being undertaken in the humanities, this area will soon be ripe for exploration.

Raymond McInnis, in his admirable book, *New Perspectives for Reference Service in Academic Libraries*, states the significance of this science of research for bibliographic instruction concisely:

> If I were asked [he writes] to name the most important

argument in this book, my immediate response would be . . . that successful and rewarding research can be conducted by students . . . in academic libraries. The provisions are that they be informed, first, of the underlying processes and practices of inquiry characteristic of particular disciplines; second, of the patterns of published research literature emanating from these activities; and third, that developing and refining research skills require thoughtful attention and deliberate practice. Three related premises are that there is a tacit logic of research strategy; that this logic can be raised to the level of awareness; and that research strategy itself can be refined by its intelligent and purposeful application.[11]

Here we have, in a nutshell, a program statement for the further development of bibliographic instruction in the 1980s.

I believe that, to realize the potential of integrated bibliographic instruction, we must eventually take two important steps. First, instruction librarians must take specialized academic training beyond the technical library science master's degree. It is the trend now in academic libraries to require an additional degree in a subject field. But I believe bibliographic instruction can best be carried out not from *within* disciplines, although subject knowledge is important, but as a *meta-discipline*, by librarians specifically trained in the interdisciplinary science of research.

Second, we need to free ourselves from the stultifying bureaucratic and technocratic mold of conventional librarianship without totally breaking the necessary practical connection of bibliographic instruction with the physical library. Those trite old phrases, "laboratory of the humanities" and "scholar's workshop," should, in fact, be straightforwardly descriptive of the library of the future.

There is one institution – Sangamon State University library in Illinois – that has been experimenting for a decade with an administrative structure designed to foster bibliographic instruction. It has a group of librarian-teachers, organized as an academic department, who are responsible for all bibliographic instruction and consultative reference activity, for collection building, and for liaison activities with other academic departments. Technical and administrative activities are handled through a regular line organization responsible directly to the head librarian. The library faculty sometimes serve as consultants on technical matters, but they have no line responsibilities or authority whatsoever.[12]

I do think that instruction librarians either must somehow transform academic libraries into supportive environments for integrated bibliographic instruction or must clearly differentiate themselves organizationally along the lines of the Sangamon State model. Since technical and administrative problems are real and persistent, strong administrative structures will continue to be needed to cope with them. Organizational differentiation seems, then, to be our likeliest safeguard against domination of the truly academic component of library services by the administrative and technical components.

IV.

The push that I see occurring now toward differentiating bibliographic instruction from the rest of academic librarianship is three-pronged. First, there is the matter of work style, which is at odds with the dominant bureaucratic institutional structure. Second, there is the matter of mission, which is at odds with the dominant technocratic value structure. In both these areas, dissonance between the instruction librarian and the prevailing ethos of academic librarianship tends to increase with the move toward integrated bibliographic instruction. Third, there is the matter of the theoretical base, which really becomes necessary and applicable only when bibliographic instruction is conducted in the integrated mode.

There will, of course, be opposition, complete with charges of intellectual pretention, elitism, and violation of the essential nature of librarianship. A recent example is an article by Pauline Wilson. She argues that librarians who claim to be teachers are guilty of an "organization fiction" concocted to counter the unflattering stereotype of the librarian, to enhance their status, and to give their occupation a label that will make it seem more intelligible to outsiders. Wilson defines the essence of librarianship as the dissemination of physical library materials, not their contents, and she warily approves instruction of users in access techniques as a legitimate dissemination activity. But she suspects that the bibliographic instruction movement, on the whole, is a ploy of strongly career-oriented librarians (an attitude, by the way, of which she disapproves) to obtain faculty status. She admits her real concern, that ALA will be weakened by the possible establishment of ACRL as an independent organization, only as a coda to her argument.[13]

The opposing forces in librarianship today, of differentiation on the one hand and conformity on the other, can best be understood by contrasting two approaches to the sociology of professions. The traditional approach, which is incorporated in most of the literature I have seen on librarianship as a profession, attempts to define and analyze the concept "profession" in order to classify various occupations according to their positions along a continuum of increasing professionalization. This is the approach taken, for instance, in the frequently quoted article by William Goode in which he concluded that librarianship is not and never will be a true profession.[14] It is an approach which, in order to classify occupations, necessarily simplifies them into discrete unities, giving the impression that they enjoy a high degree of internal coherence and are contained by strict outer boundaries.

In the same year that Goode's article was published (1961), Bucher and Strauss introduced an alternative model -- a "process" or "emergent" view of professions.[15] It is applicable, I think, to any occupation that defines itself in terms of a professional mission. It sidesteps completely the question of classification of occupations and looks, instead, at the internal dynamics of professional groups. In contrast to the traditional "functionalist" view of professions as discrete unities, it looks upon a profession as a "loose amalgamation [of interest groups] pursuing different objectives in different manners . . . under a common name at a particular period in history."[16]

These interest groups, called segments, are miniature social movements. Like religious, political, or reform movements in the larger society, they emerge, develop, are modified, and, having wrought changes in the profession as a whole, may eventually merge again into the parent group. A segment is distinguished during its lifetime by its sense of unique mission, its particular conception of the most characteristic professional act, its conception of the ideal client relationship, and usually the formation of its own professional associations. Its chosen alliances may indicate, even, that it has more in common with a neighboring occupation than with its own parent profession. Since professions function within institutional situations, "a large part of the activity of segments is a power struggle for the possession of [institutions] or some kind of place within them."[17]

Clearly, there is considerable evidence that instruction librarians are now engaged in that segmenting process. We are differentiating ourselves -- attitudinally, intellectually, and organizationally -- from a profession that is trying its best to contain us in the organizational fold while declaring our ultimate intellectual mission to be out of bounds. To see this drama in the framework of a sociological analysis of professions will not change the motives of either side. But the knowledge that professional differentiation is a normal, continuous social process should completely legitimize our attempt to redefine academic librarianship. It should reassure us that our dissonant personal style serves noble ends. It may encourage us, moreover, to think adventurously about the prospects for bibliographic instruction during the 1980s and beyond.

NOTES

1. Mary Mancuso Biggs, "The Perils of Library Instruction," *Journal of Academic Librarianship* 5(1979):159.

2. Ibid., p. 162.

3. Anne Beaubien, Mary George and Sharon Hogan, "Things We Weren't Taught in Library School: Some Thoughts to Take Home," in *Putting Library Instruction in Its Place: In the Library and in the Library School*; papers presented at the Seventh Annual Conference on Library Orientation for Academic Librarians, Eastern Michigan University, May 12–13, 1977, ed. by Carolyn A. Kirkendall (Ann Arbor, Michigan: Pierian Press, 1978), pp. 71–84.

4. Joseph A. Boissé, "Library Instruction and the Administration," in *Putting Library Instruction in Its Place*, p. 3.

5. Nancy E. Gwinn, "Academic Libraries and Undergraduate Education: The CLR Experience," *College & Research Libraries* 41(1980):11.

6. Kay Rottsolk, letter to the author, February 1, 1980.

7. Gwinn, p. 7. The main report of this experimental program is in Patricia B. Knapp, *Monteith College Library Experiment* (New York: Scarecrow Press, 1966).

8. Virginia H. Parr, "Faculty Liaison: A Departmental Model in Psychology," paper presented at the program of the ACRL Education and Behavioral Sciences Section, annual meeting of the American Library Association, Dallas, Texas, June 25, 1979.

9. Jon Lindgren, "Seeking a Useful Tradition for Library User Instruction in the College Library," in *Progress in Educating the Library User*, ed. by John Lubans, Jr. (New York: Bowker, 1978), pp. 71–91.

10. All these terms have been used as labels for a new social science that studies knowledge, but their definitions, of course, are not identical. "Social epistemology" is Jesse Shera's term. See, for example, his "The Role of the College Librarian – A Reappraisal," in *The Role of the College Library – A Reappraisal in Library-Instructional Integration at the College Level*; report of

the 40th Conference of Eastern College Librarians (Chicago: Association of College Reference Librarians, 1955), p. 10. "Episto-dynamics" comes from Manfred Kochen, "Stability in the Growth of Knowledge," *American Documentation* 20(1969): 195. "Catenics" was coined by Alan R. Taylor, "A Model for Academic Library Service," in *Papers Delivered at the Indiana University Library Dedication*, Bloomington Campus, October 9–10, 1970 (Bloomington, Indiana: Indiana University Library, 1971), p. 19. "Informatics" is used in D.A. Kemp, *The Nature of Knowledge: An Introduction for Librarians* (London: Clive Bingley, 1976), p. 173. "Science of research" comes from Glynn Harmon, "Opinion Paper on the Evolution of Information Sciences," *ASIS: Journal of the American Society for Information Science* 22 (1971):240, as cited in Raymond G. McInnis, *New Perspectives for Reference Service in Academic Libraries* (Westport, Connecticut: Greenwood Press, 1978), p. xix.

11. Raymond G. McInnis, *New Perspectives for Reference Service*, p. xx.

12. Breivik, Patricia Senn, "A Model for Library Management," in *Personnel in Libraries*, ed. by Karl Nyren (Library Journal Special Report, No. 10, 1979), pp. 4–9. Although the organizational structure described here will probably be altered under new management, the fact that it survived for a decade means that it will continue to serve as an important model for academic libraries of the future.

13. Pauline Wilson, "Librarians as Teachers: The Study of an Organization Fiction," *Library Quarterly* 49(1979):146–162.

14. William Goode, "The Librarian: From Occupation to Profession?" *Library Quarterly* 31(1961):306–318.

15. Rue Bucher and Anselm Strauss, "Professions in Process," *American Journal of Sociology* 66(1961):325–334.

16. Ibid., p. 326

17. Ibid., p. 333.

POLITICS AND PERSONALITIES: A PANEL

Judith Avery, University of Michigan
Roger W. Fromm, Bloomsburg State College
Bonnie J. King, University of Toledo
Cerise Oberman--Soroka, College of Charleston
Virginia Tiefel, Ohio State University

THE CHALLENGE OF THE 80s

Judith Avery

A month ago I could have told you why instruction librarians are young -- they die off before they can get old from an overdose of freshman English. I was almost there myself, but now that the semester is over, I'm able to look at the question in a more analytical light.

First let me say that I'm not all sure it is true that instruction librarians are young. Speaking personally, I had seen the first blush of youth go from these cheeks some time before I taught my first class. But, undeterred by my reservations about the truth of the assertion that instruction libraries are young, I will proceed to give you my unsubstantiated reasons for this disputed fact. Meanwhile I trust you to keep in mind what I always tell our freshmen -- just because someone says it, doesn't make it so; even if you read it in a book.

Let me talk first about two parallel trends of the past ten to fifteen years. Now you may also warn your freshmen (and someone ought to) that chronological juxtaposition does not necessarily indicate a cause and effect, or, indeed, any kind of relationship. But disregarding that for a moment, let us assume that these two trends are somehow related.

Trend One: In the middle sixties, as some of us here remember, there was a shortage of librarians. By 1970 that was no longer true. The employment picture for the seventies, especially the early years, was grim. Neither the young librarian just leaving school nor the seasoned veteran looking for a change could be confident of finding an appropriate opening. Those who had jobs tended to stay in them.

Trend Two: A segment of the library community, mostly young, began a renaissance in library instruction. Library instruction had always been there, but in the late sixties and early seventies it received new attention. As indicators of this let me remind you that the first National Conference on Library Instruction was held here in Ypsilanti in 1971 and that LOEX, BIS, and LIRT are all products of the 1970s.

It is my contention that the upsurge of interest in library instruction and the relative youth of its practitioners are directly related to the constricting of job opportunities in librarianship.

Unlike some professions, librarianship is hierarchical. A dentist advances not by becoming some higher level of dentist — assistant dentist, associate dentist, full dentist -- but by accumulating more, or wealthier, patients. Librarians, on the other hand, generally rise by moving to jobs requiring more, or a different sort of, responsibility. In the 1970s this opportunity for upward movement was decidedly curtailed. The higher level jobs were not available in quantities sufficient to meet the numbers either already in or entering the profession.

When the opportunity to rise went so did the challenge of new, more responsible jobs. Few beginning level jobs are, unchanged, able to long challenge the talented and ambitious individual. So in the seventies some of these talented librarians found alternatives to the career ladder climb to invest their talents and energies in.

Library instruction. It waxes and wanes as an interest of the library profession. Those years of the late sixties with the greater emphasis in education on individual intellectual pursuits and the large library population lacking the needed research skills, were an ideal time for a resurgence of instruction. And there were numbers of frustrated young librarians eager to put their energies into it.

In most cases the early library instruction programs came from the bottom up: librarians in entry-level jobs initiated the programs or greatly enhanced existing programs. They were the ones close enough to the users to see the need. They were the ones with the enthusiasm and the creative energies needing an outlet.

Administrators quickly saw library instruction as a good thing. Having a program made the library look good both within the profession, where instruction had become the thing to do, and within the institution, where it was seen as being responsive to user needs. And, in the beginning at least, it could be done at so little cost; librarians were willing to take it on in addition to regular duties.

The administrators granted instruction librarians more freedom than junior members in our profession often get. Since they had never done instruction themselves, or even thought about it, there was no one to quash enthusiasm with a "but we've always done it that way" or a "we tried that and it didn't work." Although money was generally a problem, traditional practices were not, since most libraries' instruction programs were so minimal that they could easily be integrated into whatever new was done. And there were so many possibilities! Workbooks and handbooks and programmed textbooks. Maxicourses and minicourses and one-hour stands. Programs for minorities, for faculty, for subject specialists. Audiotapes and videotapes and computer tapes. Signs and term paper clinics and point-of-use. Enough to keep even the most enthusiastic and energetic librarian engaged.

These librarians banded together in BIS and LIRT and exchanged ideas through LOEX; I've mentioned the recent founding of all of these. The early members of these groups were not people who had studied bibliographic instruction in library school to be hired for an instruction job. They were librarians who had built their own programs, often from scratch. They were people who in another day would have been running libraries. Lacking the opportunity for that, they created their own instruction programs. For some few of them this has meant success in a traditional framework. Some have moved from instruction to traditional career ladder positions. Some have risen to national offices in the previously mentioned library instruction interest groups. Some have created programs sufficiently complex to need other librarians in jobs subordinate to theirs, that is, they created their own hierarchies.

That for the recent past. What of today? Today in many places library instruction openings are still near the entry level. Administrative attitudes, perhaps formed by the youth of those who initiated programs, often decree this to be a job for the beginner. But not the rank beginner. A question I am constantly asked by library science students is "Where can I get some experience in library instruction?" They tell me that listings even for beginning level jobs ask for experience and/or course work in instruction. And those beginning jobs now often report to other librarians, who direct the work. No more the young librarian who builds from enthusiasm and talent? Has the question become not "Why are instruction librarians young?" but "Are we in danger of becoming old?" Are we seeing an aging phenomenon caused by the "credentializing" and "bureaucratizing" of what has so recently been a young, dynamic field?

Library instruction has made enormous gains in the last decade. In national conferences like this one and in the constantly growing body of literature, we are able to learn from the research and from the successes and failures of people established in the field. "Established," in fact, is the word for bibliographic instruction these days. It is as much a part of librarianship as cataloging or rare books or reference. It has its own organizations, its own spokespeople, its own hierarchies.

What it cannot afford, however, is its own definition of how the job is to be done. There is no right way to do instruction. Library instruction needs the enthusiasm of the young today as much as it did in 1970. And it needs those young librarians to be given free enough rein to make their own mistakes -- and create their own successes. It would be a pity if instruction became so codified, so much a part of a hierarchy, that innovation was discouraged. In the 1970s young librarians found an outlet for their creative talents in instruction; the challenge for the 1980s is to keep this opportunity open.

TUESDAY MORNING LIVE -- PERSONALITY AND BIBLIOGRAPHIC INSTRUCTION

Roger W. Fromm

The success of library instruction depends 90 percent on the personality of the librarian. We might quibble about the percent, but it seems that the general notion is true if we accept one of the following common dictionary definitions of personality:
 1. The sum total of the physical, mental, emotional and social characteristics of an individual.
 or 2. The organized pattern of behavioral characteristics of an individual.

Whether we accept the first definition or the second, not much is left out of what a person uses in presenting some material for intellectual consideration. We assume for our library instruction librarian the intelligence and education necessary to obtain a professional position in an academic library.

My premise is that effective teaching comes from the same elements whatever the academic department. In reading about college teaching, nowhere did I find evidence that would contradict the notion that personality plays the largest role in determining teaching effectiveness. In fact, educators concerned about effective teaching at any level come back to the basic personality of the teacher as the important factor.

Educational theorists and psychologists have pointed this out. Charles Skinner in his *Essentials of Educational Psychology* notes that studies of teaching success eventually emphasize "the somewhat intangible factor of the teacher's personality."[1] Young and Pullias in their book, *A Teacher Is Many Things*, state that although the qualities of personality are difficult to illustrate, the effectiveness of a teacher is greatly influenced by his personal qualities as reflected in attitudes toward himself, the students, and learning.[2] And others have discovered that the personal style in communicating is the important difference in teaching results.

What are the personality characteristics that make the difference? Scholars have been teaching literature, philosophy, chemistry, etc. for decades. We can look at their experience to determine something about the teaching/learning process. Most of them mention the following:

confidence enthusiasm empathy
sense of humor imagination emotional stability

Robert Segal, professor of religion and humanities at Reed College, says emotional qualities are the most important in good teaching; he cites compassion, enthusiasm, and humor as crucial.[3] A good sense of humor seems a quality appearing on everybody's list. Gilbert Highet in his classic, *The Art of Teaching*, says humor keeps students alive and attentive, and, more importantly, it hooks the student and teacher together -- people who laugh together work better together. And humor makes the teacher's authority more palatable.[4]

The instructor is on stage sending messages through his appearance, voice, and body language. Confidence, a sense of humor, enthusiasm, and imagination are needed to act in front of 25 students. An actor persuades the audience that he is the character portrayed; similarly, says Wayne DeLozier of the University of South Carolina, a professor must convince students that his subject is important to them.[5]

A number of contributors to a 1975 book of essays, *Excellence in University Teaching*, sees enthusiasm as the sine qua non of teaching.[6] We must, they say, have or be able to feign enthusiasm for whatever we're attempting to teach; the point is – you cannot expect to get students interested if you don't show great interest yourself. Commenting on enthusiasm and the dramatic, one professor admits that "students who have praised my teaching for enthusiasm, sincerity, openness never suspected the theatrical . . . in it – or maybe they did. Does it matter? Their 'belief' in me is a means to an end."

All of this requires confidence and a demeanor that expresses some of that confidence. This, of course, is needed when we look down a row and catch a student's facial expression that suggests the blase approach of an Oscar Wilde. Oscar Wilde, upon returning to England after visiting the United States, was asked how he liked Niagara Falls. In his own inimitable fashion, Wilde replied that he would have been more impressed if the water had flown the other way. There are some students who are hard to impress.

A word of caution before we turn to library instruction per se. There is no one right style of teaching. Perhaps the most we can say is that an instructor should use a style consonant with his own personality. Yet, as someone has said, teaching is a personal *but* not a private act. We might have to make an adjustment here or there.

If we accept the notion that personality is a very significant factor in teaching effectiveness, then my contention is that this applies especially in the case of library instruction.

First of all, the library instructor may have to counteract the image that librarians have had for years. There have been some extraordinary, persistent, and, in some cases, even outrageous efforts in recent years to mitigate the traditional image. Despite this, vestiges of it remain. There is much evidence to show that a reputation once established is difficult to overcome. Related to this is any reputation carried from our reference desk work to the classroom. The personality exhibited in reference had better not be negative because the impression given is enduring. Any contrary evidence (such as good teaching) will have to go through the very tough sieve of student consciousness of previous impressions.

Carrying this notion a step further, compounding our problem is that most of us have the students before us for a very short time – some for only 50 minutes and most for a far shorter time than instructors in other departments. There is not much opportunity for students to develop an appreciation for our knowledge or whatever else that might overcome a dislike or indifference to our personality. And then frequently the students met are freshmen or sophomores working out their English composition requirements. The nature of these younger students is not to make a considered judgment of our education and expertise and balance it against their reaction to our personality.

Related to all this is student perception that there is nothing inherently interesting about library instruction. Students do not approach it in the same way they take courses in child psychology, American short story, or microbiology. And very often, more often than not I have read, the students are captive to library instruction in the sense that another professor has invited one of us into her classroom. The point is that if personality is important in the usual case it is even more important in these circumstances.

Finally, in a broad sense, the personality of the librarian determines to some extent what instructional approach is used in presenting material. There is no one best approach, but there are some approaches less effective than others.

Well, what is the message here? Should we all run out to personality school? That possibility is beyond the purview of this paper. However, I think all of us should be aware of the importance of personality in the classroom. In a more concrete fashion, I would recommend the following:

1. If you are in charge of a library use instruction program -- utilize those librarians with the most appropriate teacher personality.
2. Think twice before bringing in the cataloger to teach about the card catalog just because he is the intellectual expert. Of course, it could be that the cataloger has the best teaching personality on the staff.
3. If you're on a search and screen committee -- if library instruction is to be part of the job, look for someone with an appropriate teaching personality.

NOTES

1. Skinner, Charles E. *Essentials of Educational Psychology.* Englewood Cliffs, NJ: Prentice–Hall, 1958.

2. Pullias, Earl V. and James D. Young. *A Teacher is Many Things.* Bloomington: Indiana University Press, 1968.

3. Segal, Robert. "What Is Good Teaching? And Why Is There So Little of It?" *The Chronicle of Higher Education*, XIX (September 24, 1979), p.21.

4. Highet, Gilbert. *The Art of Teaching.* New York: Alfred A. Knopf, 1954.

5. DeLozier, M. Wayne. "The Teacher as Performer: The Art of Selling Students on Learning," *Contemporary Education*, LI (Fall, 1979), pp. 19–25.

6. Buxton, Thomas H. and Keith W. Prichard, eds. *Excellence in University Teaching: New Essays.* Columbia: University of South Caroline Press, 1975.

A LIBRARIAN FOR ALL SEASONS

Bonnie J. King

I feel that the success of an orientation and instruction activity does depend 90% on the personality of the librarian developing and administering the program.

In reading the literature on librarianship, the negative "old maid" image of the librarian often surfaces. Personality traits that have been associated with this stereotype are orderliness, conservatism and conformity. The image also suggests that the librarian lacks vigor, ambition, imagination and is introspective rather than outgoing.

The bibliographic instruction librarian usually exhibits personality traits that are completely opposite the characteristics listed in the above stereotypes. The beginning instructor-librarian is often creative, innovative, a self-starter and is full of enthusiasm, courage, motivation and drive. However, these qualities may also be perceived as a negative stereotype.

In reviewing "the old maid" versus "the ball of fire" stereotype, I find neither of these images satisfactory. I feel that a flexible, balanced set of personality characteristics is necessary to create and maintain a successful bibliographic instruction program.

Personality skills that I have found essential in producing an effective bibliographic instruction program are good communication, careful planning, promotion, feedback-revision and patience.

The bibliographic instruction librarian first must be a good communicator and listener. Since activities often begin with ideas that are casually mentioned by the faculty and administrator, it is up to the librarian to interpret, develop and project the concepts into workable projects.

Poor communication is the prime area of difficulty between librarians and the faculty. Often classroom faculty are unaware of library services, problems and procedures. On the other hand, librarians often are unaware of curriculum developments and needs.

How can this communication gap be successfully bridged? Written communications that serve as an introduction to services offered and a "user needs survey" could be a beginning information step. However, face-to-face personal contact with individual faculty members and departments heads has produced the most significant rapport, continued communication and commitment to new programs in bibliographic instruction. The success of these face-to-face personal contacts emphasizes the personality characteristics of the good bibliographic instruction librarian.

The individual in the bibliographic instruction position displays the characteristic of being a good planner and organizer. He or she needs a working familiarity with administrative and university needs, as well as with university organization and structure to be able to develop activities that are relevant and appropriate.

The bibliographic instruction librarian is a good promoter and sales person. In introducing programs to the faculty, administration, students and other librarians, the bibliographic instruction librarian is persuasive, a "polite pusher" with an attitude of interest and empathy.

The development of harmonious interpersonal relationships is vital and the bibliographic instruction librarian must be capable of cultivating these. A librarian must be a whiz at public relations. The bibliographic instruction librarian has a wealth of important contacts that can be of great significance to the university. The instructors, department heads, administrators, students, librarians, other universities and the community are all in contact with the bibliographic instruction librarian. In all of these contacts, he or she represents the university and can do so much to enhance the library's image as a high-quality, caring, well managed institution.

The librarian as a teacher needs to be a stimulus to the students, capable of generating from them in a short period of time an interest in information and in the access to resources that are readily available.

The bibliographic instruction librarian gives personalized service to all users making them feel that their requests are important and that they are also. Part of rendering this personal service is being able to converse comfortably and intelligently with users.

This personalized service reinforces the earlier mentioned necessity for good communication. Feedback obtained from students, instructors and librarians in reference desk communication aids in research, collection development and in the revision and future planning of bibliographic instruction materials and programs.

After feedback and revision, patience is a key personality trait. A delicate balance needs to be maintained between enough communication and enthusiasm to maintain the change effort of bibliographic instruction in the face of resistance and not so much enthusiasm that careful planning and feedback are overlooked. This may be the point in the program where demand for service creates the need for media systems and self-guided programs. Well designed instructional systems can balance the planning and patience need while reflecting the personality influence of the creating librarian.

In closing, a bibliographic instruction librarian must be a special, unique kind of person who is flexible and able to operate and think on multiple tracks. Many things will be happening simultaneously. The librarian will at one time or another serve as a teacher, researcher, reference librarian, collection developer, strategist, administrator, politician, writer and sage. The librarian is the single most important determinant of the quality of library services.

In bibliographic instruction, a good balance of the personality traits and skills evident in good communication, careful planning, promotion, feedback and patience is essential for a successful bibliographic instruction program. The bibliographic instruction librarian must indeed be "a man or woman for all seasons."

NOTES

Larry Hardesty, "Instructional Development in Library Use Education." *Faculty Involvement in Library Instruction*, Carolyn Kirkendall, ed (Ann Arbor: Pierian Press, 1979), pp. 11–35.

PERSONALITY TO EDUCATION: A NECESSARY CHANGE

Cerise Oberman-Soroka

The role of personality has been elevated to a height of prime importance in the bibliographic instruction movement. The result, the personality or perish dilemma, has become virtually synonymous with bibliographic instruction. We have, however, failed to recognize this problem as an underlying symptom of a far more serious issue -- the loss of a clearly defined philosophy for bibliographic instruction.

The bibliographic instruction movement has too often measured its impact by the growing number of instruction librarian positions. The creation of these positions has been the library's political focal point for infiltrating academic departments for the purpose of establishing instruction programs. We have been made well aware of the number and types of obstacles which confront the establishment of such programs. Therefore, as a strategic, if unconscious move, we have manufactured the concept of the instruction librarian. This has led to a self-defeating belief: that an outgoing, assertive, energetic, and charismatic personality can overcome the forces which block the establishment of instruction programs.

This mythology has done more damage to the bibliographic instruction movement than any other single assumption. By nurturing a separate identity for instruction librarians, and creating special, and usually separate job titles, we have made bibliographic instruction an isolationist movement. In the bureaucratic library hierarchy, isolation and segregation are a potent combination resulting in collegial mistrust, disdain, and resentment. The roadblocks, then, which an instruction program faces from within the profession are still far more serious than the obstacles from outside the profession. Because of these obstacles, no single instruction librarian can be a limitless source of strength; soon the energy evaporates, the enthusiasm dwindles, and the determination falters. What is left is a frustrated worn-out librarian who often retreats to a safer place within the profession or even abandons the profession entirely. As librarians collapse, so do programs.

We have all heard this tale of woe -- but why does it happen? If the goal of the bibliographic instruction movement is to create a separate niche for instruction within librarianship, then our expedience in developing a clique of instructional "types" should be commended. Then instruction programs will continue to be dependent on the success or failure of one person. On the other hand, if our goal is to incorporate instructional education as a basic and rudimentary principle within the discipline of librarianship, which I believe it must be, then we must assess our current methods of reaching that goal. In focusing on personality, the B.I. movement has overlooked a crucial issue: the importance of education in bibliographic instruction.

In the past, bibliographic instruction has relied too heavily on specific individuals while seeking certain personality traits to ensure a program's inception and continuation. However, education necessitates transcendance of personality; it demands a broad, comprehensive perspective of a discipline's substantive, as well as theoretical content; a grasp of the role of research within the framework of education; and an ability to demonstrate the use of the research process not as a mechanical process, but as a reasoning, thinking process. There may well be a positive correlation between personality traits and ability to instruct. What is not clear, however, is that the same personality traits insure the ability to perform as an educator.

An emphasis on education will reshape bibliographic instruction as well as librarianship. To achieve this we must consider several things. First, our attention must be turned inward. We must concentrate on what, why and how we teach. This is not to say that the practical concerns of instruction programs should be abandoned. Rather, we must focus our attention on a more comprehensive understanding of the structure of information and the way in which it is presented. Leading students to sources is only a first step. Evaluation of materials, information networking, and search processes as areas of instruction design must become integral parts of B.I.

Second, a new foundation based on theory must be laid for library education. The instruction movement must be redefined in terms of long range educational goals. As librarians we must understand and convey the complexity of our discipline to students in a clear and concise manner. Too often, in our enthusiasm to impart the value of libraries, we have neglected to insure that students have mastered the concepts which preclude the use of research methods.

Third, bibliographic education must be seen as a basic goal of librarianship, a shared responsibility, rather than the goal of a single individual or department. Involvement of colleagues, library administrators, and library school faculty is a crucial step in reshaping the B.I. movement.

Neither personality nor pedagogy alone can accomplish a shift in our present approach to bibliographic instruction. But together they can accomplish two important objectives: ridding the B.I. movement of its isolationist character, and thus, putting an end to the personality or perish syndrome; and moving librarianship as a whole closer toward fulfilling the educational function which is its base.

WHY ARE MOST INSTRUCTION LIBRARIANS YOUNG?

Virginia Tiefel

The answer is easy. They're young because library instruction requires enthusiasm, energy, commitment, and other qualities associated with youth. Or could it be that the "burn out" rate causes them to leave library instruction before they begin to age? Or have they gone on to their rewards in administrative positions where they can influence the development and direction of future programs?

My answer is none of the above because I don't subscribe to the assumption on which this question is based. Are the majority of library instruction librarians, in fact, young? Well, given the constraints of time, money, and federal regulations, we'll probably never know for certain the validity of the observation. It is, however, a very interesting question and in exploring the ramifications of the question and its answer, much is revealed about the role of the librarian in successful instruction programs. Librarians, whether young or old, tall or short, fat or thin, male or female, play a vital role in library user education. I do not mean to imply that personality is the only ingredient in successful library instruction programs, only that it is a very important factor. To succeed and endure, programs much be substantive, effective, measurable, and accountable.

Is there a relationship between personality and success? Is youth essential in successful instruction librarians? What qualities enable librarians to participate effectively in library instruction? Let's begin with the question of youth. If we can't prove that most library instruction librarians are young, can we determine if most successful programs require the characteristics commonly associated with youth? What is youth? Is it like beauty – in the eye of the beholder? Dictionaries define it as "having the appearance, freshness, vigor, or other qualities of youth" and "youthful has connotations of youth such as vigor, enthusiasm, and hopefulness." Added to these are other qualities commonly associated with "young" -- commitment, optimism, and flexibility. Are these characteristics to be found in library instruction librarians? Are they important or even relevant to the development of user education programs?

I believe they are important and offer as an example the successful program at Earlham College, where the library staff has been described by Evan Farber as flexible, eager to try new approaches and presentations, thus contributing to the flexibility and variety of Earlham's library program.[1] This certainly fits our description but this isn't all Farber says. He goes on to stress the need for librarians to be approachable, knowledgeable, and interested in students' problems. Thus the qualities associated with youth *are* important but they are not all inclusive.

Taking the broad issue of the relationship between personality and success, I searched the professional literature outside the library field for studies on their correlation. I was unable to find anything substantive, only the popular books on how to dress correctly and how to manipulate people for your own gain. There are, however, in the recent news, two good examples of the importance in knowing how to relate well to people -- which is the essence of personality. One item dealt with the firing of the chairman of a large bank in Chicago. Robert Abboud was fired from his quarter of a million dollar a year job because his style was "abrasive and autocratic." A bank spokesman said "that although the bank respected Mr. Abboud's ability as a banker, it wanted someone with greater people skills."[2]

Another kind of example can be found in a recent issue of the Sunday *New York Times Magazine*.[3] The feature story focused on Sherry Lansing who at the age of 35 had been appointed head of the 20th Century Fox Studio -- a very prestigious and powerful position. The reporter interviewed a number of people who had worked with her in her rapid rise to the top. She was described as enthusiastic, creative, intelligent, well liked, and respected. She obviously has the "people skills" not found in the Chicago banker.

If we can assume there is a relationship between the personality of instruction librarians and successful programs, what are the determining personality characteristics? It is widely recognized that collaboration with faculty is a cornerstone of every library instruction program and that the success of any program is in direct ratio to the degree of faculty support. Patricia Knapp has stated that, "we [librarians] must work primarily with and through the faculty."[4] Therefore, the ability to relate well to people is essential in an effective instruction librarian. The need to convince faculty, staff, and administrators of the importance of library instruction requires that librarians have good communication skills. This is substantiated over and over in the literature and recently by Nancy Gwinn in an article in *College and Research Libraries*.[5] In surveying the recipients of

CLR grants, Ms. Gwinn concluded that " . . . building faculty relations -- getting out of the library and into campus affairs -- is still the key to building support for the library's instructional program and other services."

Other necessary qualities are identified by Patricia Knapp who has stated that librarians should let faculty know in "an aggressive but diplomatic way that the library staff is willing and able to help them with their teaching."[6] She found that librarians are often more knowledgeable about learning theory than faculty, but must be "circumspect" about making faculty aware of it. She said that librarians must become involved in any way possible with curriculum study and reform.

A.P. Marshall has stated that librarians are now recognized as educators with valuable ideas to contribute. He urges librarians to provide innovative ideas that will contribute to the vitality in education and, like Patricia Knapp, urges them to become involved in the long-range planning processes of their institutions.[7]

What are some of the major considerations in the education and recruitment of future library instruction librarians? Lester Asheim suggests requirements for admission to library school might include complete courses in communication skills and the psychology of interpersonal relations.[8] Patricia Knapp urged the recruitment of librarians who have the qualifications to collaborate actively with the teaching faculty, e.g., a commitment to teaching, broad liberal arts background and a thorough understanding of curriculum design, learning theory, and instructional methods.[9] Abell and Passarelli found the quality of programs dependent on the resourcefulness and originality of the staff and advocated that staff be recruited with this in mind.[10] John Berry noted, "Crucial to the rebirth of libraries is their ability to attract and employ new talent. This doesn't necessarily mean youthful talent, although it can."[11]

Thus youth, while not an undesirable feature, is not essential; the important qualities of a good library instruction librarian are ageless. They are diplomacy, initiative, innovation, knowledge, empathy, flexibility, skill in relating to people and in effective communication. In addition, enthusiasm, energy, and commitment, while associated with youth, are not confined to the young.

One thing is certain in my mind, though, if library instruction librarians have all of the above, they will not only contribute to the educational goals of their institutions and to their profession, they will surely lead fuller, richer lives.

NOTES

1. Farber, Evan Ira. "Library Instruction throughout the Curricu-

lum: Earlham College Program," John Lubans, editor, *Educating the Library User*. (NY: Bowker, 1974):pp. 155–156.

2. Rout, Lawrence, "First Chicago Chairman Abboud Is Fired," *Wall Street Journal*, (April 29, 1980):p.12.

3. Schulberg, Budd, "What Makes Hollywood Run Now?" *New York Times Magazine*, (April 27, 1980): pp.52–88.

4. Knapp, Patricia B., "Guidelines for Breaking the System: A Strategy for Moving toward the Ideal of the Undergraduate Library as a Teaching Instrument," *Drexel Library Quarterly*, (July–October 1971): p.219.

5. Gwinn, Nancy E., "Academic Libraries and Undergraduate Education: The CLR Experience," *College and Research Libraries* 41 (January 1980): p.10.

6. Knapp, "Guidelines for Breaking," p.218.

7. Marshall, A.P. "The Teaching/Learning Thing: Librarians as Educators," in *Academic Libraries by the Year 2000*. Herbert Poole, editor, (NY: Bowker, 1977): pp.50–63.

8. Asheim, Lester, "Education of Future Academic Librarians," in *Academic Libraries by the Year 2000*. Herbert Poole, editor. (NY: Bowker, 1977): pp.128–138.

9. Knapp, "Guidelines for Breaking," p.220.

10. Passarelli, Anne and Millicent D. Abell. "Problems of Undergraduate Libraries and Problems in Educating Library Users," in *Educating the Library User*. John Lubans, editor (NY: Bowker, 1974): p.126.

11. Berry, John, "Problems of Maturity," *Library Journal*. (January 1, 1976) p.13.

BIBLIOGRAPHIC INSTRUCTION IN THE 1980s AND BEYOND

Michael Keresztesi
Wayne State University

I would like to speak to the central theme of this conference and share with you my belief in a bright future for bibliographic instruction in the coming decade and beyond. My optimism is based on a variety of new developments in the field of higher education and on some new approaches in the scientific and scholarly disciplines as well, all of which are creating a favorable climate for our efforts to disseminate bibliographic literacy in academic libraries.

The general trend to maximize the utilization of existing resources in colleges and universities is such a development. Bibliographic instruction is beginning to be seen as a method of teaching people how to utilize more effectively the library's resources. Even outside the university, one cannot fail to notice the increasing attention that some professional associations, notably historians, economists, and political scientists, have been giving in recent years to the improvement of their bibliographical equipment. The establishment last year of the Association for the Bibliography of History signals the intense preoccupation of American historians with bibliography.

Our success in disseminating bibliographic literacy in the 1980's will be largely determined by the degree we can take advantage of the opportunities offered by the new climate in the field, and by our ability to elevate the methods of bibliographic instruction to higher levels of sophistication. The need for more sophisticated approaches arises from the fact that our drive for bibliographic literacy must begin with the advanced researcher, including the faculty. For this reason, the focus of this paper is that segment of the university constituency which is routinely involved in research: graduate students, the professional researcher, and the faculty. Only in partnership with the faculty can we generate on our campuses an environment conducive to the growth of bibliographic culture. "Bibliographic culture" is a condition in which genuine respect for the library prevails, its resources are creatively utilized for all educational, research, cultural, and recreational activities, and librarians are accepted as equal partners in a joint intellectual enterprise.

But there are forces which inhibit the realization of these objectives. Among them, we should pay particular attention to latent and overt antagonism between librarians and the scientific community on the campuses. It is my intention to discuss the conceptual aspects underlying this antagonism with a view not only to understanding the problem, but also using the insights gained in the exploration of their implications for library instruction.

The first source of difficulty can be traced to the difference in orientation, from which the two communities -- librarians on the one hand, scientists, researchers, and scholars, on the other -- derive their value system. Librarians tend toward generality, breadth, surface manifestations, topography, and communication. The practitioners of scientific disciplines, on the other hand, move toward specialization, territoriality, substance, depth and structure, narrowness, and methodology. Librarians, as a rule, don't dig into a subject; they are tuned to the surface manifestations of a discipline's literature, such as format, provenance, and chronological aspects, and are concerned with the content *only* to the extent that it can be compressed for convenient storage, and expressed in an index term for easy retrieval. The librarian's relationship to the disciplines's terrain is that of a ranger, not of the geologist's. But who could denigrate the ranger's knowledge of the topography when we are looking for a lost child in a national forest?

Another source of the antagonism may be attributed to the competing concerns of librarians and the subject-oriented reseachers for the records and the information apparatus of the respective scientific disciplines. "Information apparatus" denotes the entirety of reference tools and bibliographic equipment, manual and mechanical, which comes into existence to serve the needs of the discipline.

The two groups, librarians and researchers, relate to the records in a different manner, which can be partially explained by divergencies in their professional preparation. The researcher or faculty member is trained in graduate school to be practitioner, which involves application, concrete problem-solving, research and teaching; all three requiring substantive and structural uses of records as well as the enlargement of the records by the faculty member's own professional contributions.

Librarians, on the other hand, are trained to acquire, assemble, organize, and preserve those records; operations which may seem to the scholarly or scientific practitioner as merely manipulative, or even parasitic. What may also irk the practitioner is the notion that someone external to the discipline exercises patrimony over the intellectual materials belonging to those who create and utilize them.

Further difficulties may arise from the mode of inquiry and the way librarians and the scholarly community approach an information problem and the way they solve it. The approach of librarians is morphological, that is, arrangement by category. This is due to the librarians' indoctrination in library schools in categorizing and thinking in terms of types of reference tools when seeking answers to questions.

For scientists and scholarly researchers this method usually will not do. The scientist's information needs are etiological, that is, they are caused by a research problem at hand; they are embedded in the subject matter under study and cannot be easily isolated into neat units. Scientists are not generally familiar with bibliographic and reference typology and the titles of reference publications given by their publishers are often no help to the scholar trying a morphological approach. The whimsical manner in which bibliographic nomenclature is being used to designate reference works, makes the morphological approach confusing for the uninitiated. Even to the highly sophisticated outsider, the bewildering array of bibliographic tools and reference works does not appear as a coherent systematic universe with an internally logical order and with linkages on many different tiers. For these reasons, an attempt to present and to explain the bibliographical universe to the scientific researcher as a morphological system, can be an exercise in frustration.

And this is the issue. The bibliographical education of the researcher requires new conceptual tools. To construct such tools we must first redefine for ourselves as well as for "outsiders" the concept of bibliography.

The traditional meaning of bibliography connotes inventorial and descriptive efforts on various levels regarding published materials. We believe this interpretation is too narrow and incongruous with the actual interests of the field. A more meaningful view is that bibliography is itself an intellectual pursuit concerned with how knowledge is generated, organized, formatted, packaged and communicated; and how and what kind of reference and bibliographic works come into existence as products or instrumentalities of the process of knowledge generation.

Thus, bibliography becomes the total information apparatus of a discipline, in the same sense as tanks, helicopters, batteries, and other pieces of armory constitute the logistical support system of an army on the move. To study the bibliography of a discipline means to study access to its literature on the one hand, and to analyze, describe, evaluate, and interpret the information apparatus of that discipline in light of the logistical objectives it is called on to serve. To understand this approach it is useful to make a functional analysis of the structure of scientific disciplines.

Scientific and scholarly disciplines may be described in functional terms as knowledge producing and knowledge disseminating systems, based in the academia. This definition has several implications; first, that the reason for a discipline's existence is the production of knowledge in that parcel of reality which it has staked out for itself; secondly, that new knowledge discovered through research, initially must be communicated to members of the profession by means of established channels and must also be accepted by it. Ultimately, new knowledge will infiltrate society in one form or another. Thirdly, this definition maintains that in order for scientific or scholarly discipline to be productive, it must gain approval by society. It receives this approval symbolically when it is allowed to move into the university. Essentially, there is no bona-fide scientific or scholarly discipline in America today outside the university.

A systemic conception of scientific disciplines displays a complex mechanism of many components, each of which has an importat role to play. Without meshing the many components into a synergistic working entity, new knowledge production would be inconceivable at our present stage of scientific and cultural development. At the center of the system stands the scientist, scholar, or researcher, individually, or as a member of a team, ready to carve out a piece of reality to observe, to experiment with, to gather data on, to establish new facts, discern new patterns, formulate new theories, and reveal new truths.

But before this process can begin, a thorough search must be made in the accumulated records, that is, the literature, of the respective discipline, to see if the projected exploration has already been accomplished, so that wasteful duplication can be avoided. The search of literature is also needed to bring to light the state of our present knowledge on the subject. It is clear, that without the physical existence of the records in libraries, and without organized access to them, provided by the bibliographical services of librarians, the research capability of a scientific discipline would be gravely impaired, if not totally obstructed.

Only after a thorough literature search, generally performed with a librarian's assistance, can the researcher move to the next stage: devising the research tools, or selecting them among existing ones. These can be works which provide the researcher with the applicable methodology, and procedure, usually embodied in manuals and handbooks; or which supply the standardized terminology, nomenclature, and formulas contained in subject dictionaries; or which place at the researcher's disposal already accumulated and systematized data, as in the case of statistical compilations. Today, most researchers are already relieved of the burden of tool-making, a task taken over by an arm of the professional association, the government, or the publishing industry. The main point here is that tool-making is an important contributory element in the system.

After pursuing new knowledge, the researcher's most important obligation is to communicate the findings and implications of his research. A variety of formalized instruments of communication has come into existence: letters, reviews, article, studies, essays, reports, conference papers, and monographs. The main vehicles are journals, magazines, bulletins, newsletters, pamphlets, numbered series, and others, which together constitute the vast intellectual circulatory system that keeps the discipline alive.

The academic, too, is part of the system. It performs three vital functions. The first relates to the professional preparation of practitioners of a discipline and the granting of socially sanctioned credentials, without which they cannot practice. The second function is organizing and institutionalizing research within the university in specialized centers, institutes, and laboratories. Attracting large government and private grants, many universities have now become veritable knowledge factories. The third is establishing channels of information dissemination. A large number of specialized journals and a huge body of scientific report literature emanate from university research centers, institutes, and academic departments, along with a stream of the conventional catalogs, syllabi, course texts, brochures, and other types of reference materials. An important vehicle for publishing activity is the university press whose main business is to provide an outlet for the narrowly focused monographic literature growing out of Ph.D. related research and for the academic writings of the faculty for which the market would be very limited.

The professional organization occupies a pivotal position in the life of a discipline. Beyond serving as a social and political arm of organized practitioners, the professional association also provides a forum, a sort of tribunal of peers, at which new research is presented, discussed, validated, or rejected. The documentary expressions of these activities are embodied in proceedings of conferences, minutes of meetings, annual reviews of literature, the official journal, the directory, and a multitude of reports by committees.

Finally, there are the funding agencies, and the contractors and consumers of research, governmental, public, private, corporate, and philanthropical, which lubricate with vast sums the wheels of our gigantic research machinery. Doing even the humblest research today is very costly. Government-sponsored research has assumed such proportions that the publishing and marketing of the scientific and technical report literature, amounting to hundreds of thousands of items, requires a special agency, the National Technical Information Service, and a distinct bibliographical mechanism to monitor it.

Viewing a scientific discipline as a knowledge producing and disseminating system has several implications for bibliographic instruction in academic libraries. First, it exhibits forcefully the partnership relationship between researcher and librarian in a joint, creative enterprise. They are both united in a common service to the discipline. Secondly, it reveals the dimensions of the role and commitment of librarians to the discipline. Developing collections for research necessitates that all documentary and literary products flowing from the activities of each component of a discipline be brought together and organized in the library for use: the bibliographic instruments and the reference tools, all communication organs, journals, reports, monographs, the publications of academic departments, the research centers, institutes, and university presses, the proceedings of meetings and conferences, the annual reviews, the reports, pertinent government documents, as well as the documents of relevant international bodies, and the profession's international umbrella organizations; in a word, every important piece of record through which the discipline as a system manifests itself. This is what constitutes a "research collection" or "collecting in depth."

Earlier we defined bibliography as a specialized information apparatus that serves the needs of a discipline. Thus, the obvious purpose of bibliographic instruction would be to acquaint the advanced researcher with this apparatus, enabling him or her to marshall all available resources that would promote the work at hand. The traditional morphological approach, that is, the preparation of a long list of reference materials by type, is not the most productive, because instead of presenting to the researcher a unified view and conceptual picture of bibliographic and reference instruments, why they exist and how they function, and why they should be capable of solving his information problems, the morphological approach demands that he go and examine more and more indexes, bibliographies, reviewing media, and so on, and gain his skills cumulatively by accretion. This method is contrary to the principle of economy which scientists and scholars must respect.

Let me suggest that the study of the history of scientific disciplines offers the elements from which a conceptual model can be constructed. Such a model can provide a rationale for and unified view of bibliography. Disciplines, after all, evolve from simple beginnings at various time points in history and go through several stages in their development which could be arbitrarily designated as (1) the pioneering stage, (2) the proliferation stage, and (3) the establishment stage. Each stage is marked by certain characteristics in the discipline's social and organizational make-up, its epistemological orientation, methodological concerns, modes of communication, and the forms and quantity of the literature produced.

In the pioneering stage, when a "great man," or the "prophet" launches his movement, the thrust of his effort is to gain converts, attention, and recognition. Nowadays, such movements are more likely to be initiated by a group of dissidents who branch off from the mainstream of an established discipline. In the beginning, the followers know each other personally and communicate informally in person or by letters in an invisible college. But as followers multiply, they must formally organize. They may no longer know each other personally. This circumstance occasions the compilation and distribution of a membership roster or perhaps a more elaborate directory.

In the very beginning, the pioneers use every conceivable medium to spread the new ideas and doctrines; lectures, articles, interviews, books, or in earlier times, pamphleteering. In order to keep the band of followers together and insure ideological purity, the incipient discipline starts a bulletin or newsletter which soon grows into a journal serving as a rallying point as well as the mouthpiece of the group. At first, the journal may be ignored by indexing services, but later it is usually picked up by a "catch--all" indexing tool.

The next stage in the life of the germinating discipline comes with an increase of followers who spread over the world, forming national and international associations. Interaction among the people in the field becomes structured and formalized through meetings, conferences, and committees. There is a need now for international directories, biographical compilations, the launching of printed proceedings, the publishing of minutes, annual reports on the activities of the organizations, and perhaps the studies and reports prepared by the various committees. The total literary output becomes very large, there is excessive preoccupation with methodology, and the once unitary subject matter of the discipline breaks up into subfields, each spawning its own journals with increasingly narrow specialization. There are so many that a special indexing or abstracting service emerges to cover them. Along with the journals, the monographic literature proliferates as well, giving rise to highly focused subject bibliographies. With the many disparate contributions and the uncoordinated use of terminology, semantic confusion may arise, requiring the standardization of usage and nomenclature by means of approved dictionaries of the discipline. The time may have come to establish the state-of-the-art, or perhaps synthesize the existing knowledge and achievements in an ambitious subject encyclopedia.

The main effort in this stage is directed toward gaining scientific legitimacy which paves the way to the university. When the discipline moves into the university, it achieves academic respectability and becomes part of the scientific establishment. In this stage of its development the discipline is organized into an academic department where teaching and training qualifications are rigidly formalized with structured curricula and requirements. Graduate programs are introduced with theses and dissertations, generating ultimately a string of reference tools.

The stratification of the discipline progresses, with strong departments attracting the "stars" who are now identified in biographical directories such as *Who Knows What* or the *Directory of Consultants*. Research is institutionalized in the university providing a market for grant reporting organs. The research center's or institute's library catalog which reflects a fairly comprehensive subject collection may find its way to a wider audience in the form of a commercially printed subject bibliography. Out in the commercial world some publishers and second-hand book dealers too begin to specialize and publish catalogs which are cherished instruments of bibliographers and acquisition and reference librarians.

This brief chronology points to the fact that there is an intrinsic relationship between bibliography and the evolution of scientific disciplines. It seems that for every major event and development in the structure, size, or orientation of a discipline, there are corresponding bibliographic responses. And parallel with diversification in the life of a discipline there is also a comparable trend toward the sophistication of the bibliographic apparatus. The direct relationship between the level of maturity of a discipline and the level of sophistication of bibliographic and reference tools is very clear. Tell me where the discipline is at in its development, and I will describe the bibliographic apparatus, and from it I will be able to tell what stage of evolution the discipline that it serves has reached.

Here, perhaps, we have come upon the ingredients of a theory of bibliography, because we are dealing with regularities, and recurring patterns which permit generalization. They tell us that bibliographic and reference works grow out of the specific information needs of a discipline. They are purposeful constructs calibrated to various types and levels of research problems. With this insight the jumble of indexes, abstracts, guides, bibliographies, catalogs, handbooks, dictionaries, directories, a multitude of various data compilations in the library fits into a recognizable pattern. Once they are so recognized, the user can make some sense of it all, and is aided in moving directly to the tools which are necessary to his or her specific area and level of research.

Let me summarize, then, the direction bibliographic instruction will take in the eighties: it will be leading to a higher plateau, to a qualitatively different understanding of the organization of the "information apparatus."

The level and sophistication of scientific disciplines and the need for rapid information delivery today have grown to such a degree that there is no longer justification for the antagonism to endure between the practitioners of a discipline and those who exercise patrimony over the recorded creations of those practitioners – the librarians. There is an obvious need for "bibliographic culture," a genuine respect for the librarian's role, and a partnership between researchers and librarians. To promote that ideal the librarian must understand the implications of viewing a discipline as a knowledge producing and disseminating system, and the researcher must be educated to the structure of bibliography as an informational apparatus.

There is no better approach to both these ends than to involve both communities in a joint effort to further develop and refine a theory of bibliography. I foresee for the eighties such a development for the ultimate benefit of everybody concerned.

POST--PRANDIAL REACTIONS: A PANEL

Suzanne Aiardo, State University of New York at Albany
Donald J. Kenney, Virginia Polytechnic Institute
and State University
Marilyn Lutzker, John Jay College of Criminal Justice
Wayne Meyer, Ball State University
Roger Sween, St. Cloud State University

THE LIBRARY ADMINISTRATOR'S
ROLE IN LIBRARY INSTRUCTION

Suzanne Aiardo

My remarks this evening are in response to the issue of why we do not read of job descriptions for library administrators that include the requirement of "commitment" as part of the job.

If one is to assume the premise that current job descriptions for library administrators do not include a statement of commitment to user education, the following theories for the omission might be offered. One could argue that commitment to user education is such a long-established hallowed tradition that it is implicit in the duties of an administrator. It is more than likely, however, and as a brief excursion through the literature has shown, that the reality is that library instruction is largely ignored or downplayed by library administrators, who seek to "keep the peace" with academic teaching faculty by not infringing on what has long been seen as the "real" faculty's territorial imperative -- the right to teach -- though at the same time the library administrators might wish to massage the egos of those grass--roots activists who believe in library instruction by allowing some informal, peripheral programs to be established.

Historically, librarians have been viewed both by themselves and others as second-class, passive members of the academic community. Pauline Wilson, I feel, clearly identifies the use, by academic librarians, of the organization fiction that librarians are teachers. This definition that librarians have of themselves may be offered as the main factor in not only limiting the effectiveness of bibliographic instruction programs, but might also be the reason for the lukewarm attitudes of library administrators towards such programs. Though I do not agree with her contention that library-use instruction cannot exist effectively without being tied to a non-library program, I agree with her postulations concerning the identity-crisis of the library profession. Academic librarians purport to be teachers because (1) they wish to dispel the unflattering stereotypes they are identified with (2) they wish to achieve status (3) they view libraries as non-integral components of the academic community so they are (4) unable to define their function or role in the university setting.[1]

An inability on the part of the academic librarians to understand and to accept librarianship as having a unique identity with meaning and dignity unto itself results in a group of people who strive to be something that they are not; who continually question their status in the academic community; and who develop programs and policies which are submissive to what are perceived to be the needs of the academic community.

The evolution of library instruction programs mirrors, to an extent, this inferiority complex we have. Though during the past decades there has been an increase in the number of credit courses offered in library instruction, the safe way out for the bibliographic instruction librarian has usually been to offer course-related instruction, which has meant seeking out and receiving the cooperation of a willing teaching faculty member. This arrangement has been successful in that it (1) does not presume to usurp the rights of the teaching faculty member; (2) it allows the librarian to interact in a more "meaningful" way with students and faculty, to be more "visible," one might say, and (3) it reinforces the concept of the librarians as passive and servile vis-a-vis the university community, therefore keeping library instruction to that level with which we were familiar in our high school days.

Though no statistical studies have clearly proven that a positive correlation exists between library use and academic achievement,[2] one might argue that a similar comparison could be made between teaching English composition and the quality of papers written for other coursework. Yet, no one questions the value of English composition as a required course in the undergraduate curriculum. But -- mention that bibliographic instruction should be a required credit course for every undergraduate, and the response, from librarians especially, is more often than not a negative one, full of credible excuses and predictable in attitude.

The proliferation of information sources and the myriad ways in which information can be retrieved make it next to impossible for anyone to use library resources intelligently without instruction. Learning about the structure and organization of knowledge and the various tools which provide the key to locations has become a saleable commodity. The enlightened consumer in the education world knows that his or her ability to obtain resources are practically limitless and extend beyond the narrow confines of the library orientation tour, or the fulfillment of the requirements of an English 100 class. While we have often heard the phrase "knowledge is power," it is now becoming equally as necessary to know *how* to obtain information.

We as bibliographic instruction librarians have a perfect opportunity at present to expand on and to solidify the gains which have been made by those grass-roots activists. The legitimacy of library instruction programs, however, can only be achieved by having the total support of library administrators. For, while it has been shown that the creation of instruction units has resulted in increased budgetary expenditures,[3] the impact of the formal integration of bibliographic instruction programs in the curricula of academic institutions can be offset by the careful scrutinizing and reassessment of reference services with an eye towards streamlining operations and redeploying staff to maximize change within fiscal constraints.

Without a firm commitment from library administrators to support and defend an independent formal program of credit offerings in bibliographic instruction, library instruction programs will never be taken seriously and librarians will continue to ride along on the coat-tails of the teaching faculty. Librarians must assume their rightful place in the academic community, and must have the support of library administrators to do so. We have not seen commitment to user education from library administrators in the past because we have not asked it of them, because we have not totally believed in it or in ourselves. They reflect our attitudes.

NOTES

1. Pauline Wilson, "Librarians as Teachers: The Study of an Organization Fiction," *Library Quarterly* 49 (April, 1979): 146–162.

2. Arthur P. Young and Exir B. Brennan, "Bibliographic Instruction: A Review of Research and Application," in John Lubans, Jr., ed., *Progress in Educating the Library User* (New York: Bowker, 1978), p. 15.

3. Allan J. Dyson, "Library Instruction in University Undergraduate Libraries," in John Lubans, Jr., ed., *Progress in Educating the Library User*, p. 101.

INSTRUCTION LIBRARIANS: BARRIERS TO INFORMATION?

Donald J. Kenney

Is knowledge in the details of conducting research *really* necessary for today's students? No, not if instructional librarians are also good informational librarians. Present trends would indicate, however that considerable interpretation and self-examination of the profession is necessary to determine if indeed we are both. To answer a question with a question – can instructional librarians be barriers to information?

Libraries, by their very nature and complexity, present numerous barriers to users. To muddy the waters, information growth is enormous, and to further magnify the problem, information systems, too, are exploding. Since the sixties, user education programs have proliferated and in many ways, though intended to make the task of finding information in a library easier, these programs can sometimes further complicate access.

Library instruction advocates are evangelical and zealous about their commitments and beliefs. Instructional librarians have risen in esteem in the library hierarchy and are gaining the respect of fellow librarians and even some administrators. We have explored and developed varied teaching techniques and teaching materials to enhance our programs. Most major information and library journals are compelled seriously to consider and to print articles dealing with bibliographic instruction and even devote entire issues to this endeavor. The movement continues to gain new converts from the neophytes entering the library profession, and even the most dubious librarians are now becoming believers. We have gained political wisdom in dealing with administrators and teaching faculty. The instructional movement, though at first confined to academic and public school libraries, is now widespread in the public sector.

We are eager to impart our knowledge about the card catalog, indexes, abstracts, and on-line information retrieval. Understandably, we seize the opportunity to teach the user some minute point of the catalog or revel in the profundities of the Library of Congress Subject Headings. Information seekers are no longer confronted with the prim, sensibly shod librarian. Instead, a vivacious librarian eagerly awaits the information seeker to explicate his need and send him happily on his way.

Our readiness and eagerness, though refreshing and commendable, is "turning off" many of our users. Just as the grim-faced reference librarian of the past was a formidable obstacle to finding information so is the new hyperenergetic instructional librarian.

The over-enthusiastic instructional librarian who captures the student who only wants an answer to a simple question and puts him through a twenty-minute library lesson drives people away from the library just as effectively as the old-fashioned reference librarian. Every student at some time or another needs information. Often, it can be obtained elsewhere -- from another student, an instructor, or the many media sources available. However, students who are pursuing a more sophisticated type of information might very well look for what they want in a library. But as librarians, and especially instructional librarians, we know most students will make a minimal effort to get the information.

Are we likely to forego this opportunity to instruct? Obviously, we have all the ingredients for an instant library lesson -- unmotivated student, information need, and a good instructional librarian. Instructional librarians have become too caught up in teaching information finding, and, consequently, the information needs of the users are neglected. The aim of libraries is to see that users get the information they seek. We should and can enable them to find it without educating them at every step.

When I want my television repaired, I call a repairman who comes to fix it. I do not expect him to arrive with wiring diagrams, assorted tubes and condensers and tools and methodically explain to me how the television set can be repaired. I can if I choose, however, take the situation under my own control and take a course in television repair.

We have forgotten that, too often, the user wants information and is not terribly intrigued how he comes by it. Many college graduates earn degrees without knowing the complexities of *Chemical Abstracts* or the logical steps of a research strategy or ever having been in the library.

What we should be concerned with is some proper balance of providing information and training. Therefore, knowledge in details of conducting research is not essential for all students today, if good instructional librarians are also good givers of information. A great deal of library instruction is rendered necessary by the complexities of the system employed by librarians. Rather than the detailed knowledge about conducting research, especially when helping the individual user, we should try to impart subtly some of the following notions:

1) information is increasing at the same rate as the literature and to cope with the increasing problem of finding what we want among a growing amount of what is not wanted, information systems are also expanding;
2) information is no longer available just in print and the user can expect to have to use a variety of media;

55

3) libraries are constantly changing and the status quo that traditionally existed can no longer be counted on;
4) critical analysis of information from varied sources should be the basis for accepting the given information;
5) users should be aware that there are numerous barriers to finding information. A great deal of time is wasted away explaining the problems of the librarian's own making. Users need to impress on librarians what they need and to work with the librarian to mold and reshape the system so that it is responsive to their needs. They help to restructure the library as they seek what they need to know and understand.
6) And finally instructional librarians need to develop a sensitivity to the situation to know when and how much instruction to provide.

IS KNOWLEDGE OF THE DETAILS
OF CONDUCTING RESEARCH REALLY NECESSARY
FOR STUDENTS TODAY?

Marilyn Lutzker

Is knowledge of the details of conducting research really necessary for students today? In my best reference-librarian manner, when faced with such a question, I'm tempted to respond with another question: Are students people? Or, at the very least, potential people, after having dropped out or graduated, or left our esteemed academic institutions? If your answer is No or even Not Really, I suspect that I might be tempted to drop my librarian's "cool" and deliver a very serious and very long lecture, so let's assume that you agree with me that students are people.

Let's look now at what we mean by research. Research, I assume we can all agree, is the search for information. But it is an experience which can be meaningful to the undergraduate on three separate levels:

(1) It enables one to gain infromation about a specific topic by learning to use the appropriate research tools and methods. This is the level which has traditionally been the focus of the teaching faculty. This is the level for the potential graduate student and the scholar.

(2) Completely aside from the subject matter involved, research is, like chess or the study of logic, an educationally meaningful experience in itself. The research process actively engages the student in the need to analyze written mate-

rial, organize ideas, think logically, and evaluate options in the search for a solution. This is the level of the well-rounded, critically thinking, humanistically educated person to which our institutions sometimes give only lip-service.

(3) Undergraduate research can provide the positive experiences, plus the general knowledge of the extent and nature of printed and computer-stored information resources which can serve a person for a lifetime. This is the level of the student as "people": as potential business manager who needs to know about security systems, industrialist who needs statistics, consumer who needs product evaluations or legal information, and of citizen who wants to know "Did so-and-so really say that?" or which community spends the most on schools, or has the least crime.

Some might argue that knowledge of the details (by which I assume one means the specifics of such complex tools as the card catalog or citation indexing) is not necessary for those whose research experiences are oriented towards the last two types. Perhaps not, for the most minimal level. But for research to be a mind-stretching experience, and a positive experience, it has to be real. A theoretical understanding of research tools and methods is absolutely essential for the type of learning I have been discussing. But the student must also somehow tangle with some of the details of the procedure before he or she can derive full benefit from the theoretical discussion.

"But," you may respond, "what is the poor instruction librarian to do when the teaching faculty has no interest in having the students do research?"

In such instances I firmly believe that the library staff -- to the extent possible -- should carry on with what they know to be a necessary component of the educational process, regardless of the level of cynicism of the faculty in other departments.

As academic librarians we are concerned with providing the broadest and most meaningful education possible for our students. If the faculty in other departments renege on their responsibilities, that is no reason why we should renege on ours. We should be teaching the students to use libraries because research in itself, regardless of subject matter, can be a learning experience for students, and because such knowledge will be of life-long help to them. Furthermore, we must convince teaching faculty that even students not destined for graduate school should be learning to use the library. We have to remind them of the value of research as a tool, and demonstrate to them that meaningful research assignments can be designed which will benefit those students.

In my own school, and I know that this is true elsewhere as well, the English department faculty, who are charged with teaching students how to write research papers, had been complaining for a long time about the exceedingly poor quality of the papers they were receiving, and were moving increasingly away from true research papers to book reports, annotated bibliographies, and the handing-in of note cards. The usual term paper assignments were either the traditional Hemingway, Billy Budd or Tom Jones criticism, or, on the part of the more "forward looking" faculty, a paper on "any topic which interests you." Translated, this latter assignment turns into seemingly hundreds and hundreds of uninspired papers on capital punishment, drug abuse and abortion, based on articles located through the *Readers' Guide*. The students were learning little about the topics that they did not already know, and were learning very little about research. Furthermore, they seemed to be almost as bored with the topics as their teachers and the library staff.

I have thought a good deal about undergraduate research projects in recent years, and not only do I believe that it is of benefit on the three levels which I have described, but I also firmly believe that most students will enjoy doing research, if the topics are well chosen and the tools and methodologies are properly explained.

Starting with my observations of what types of research the students seem to enjoy the most, and find the most challenging, I have been working with members of the English department to develop new types of research assignments, and I am happy to say that faculty report not only student enthusiasm, but a definite improvement in the quality of the papers, if not always in the spelling.

I have observed that as much as my generation dislikes microfilm, my students are happy to spend hours poring over old copies of the *New York Times*, and they are absolutely fascinated to find that in their very own school library they can read newspapers and magazines that were published more than 100 years ago. Their enthusiasm in dealing with what is basically primary source material is marvelous; it has even turned some of the cynics in the English department almost into believers.

Our second semester English course has both a literature component and a research paper component. Some faculty attempt to integrate these two; others keep them separate. Among the more successful attempts to fuse the two was a class which read fiction of World War I, including *All Quiet on the Western Front*, and then read descriptions of the battles in the *New York Times* and the *London Times*. Another class read a collection of slave narratives, and then located contemporary articles from the *Times* and various magazines describing runaway slaves and slave revolts. Other classes had gone back to newspapers and magazines of earlier times to read about burning issues which the students had never heard about – things like the Triangle Shirt Waist Fire, the Bonus Marches of the 1930's, and the Armory show which introduced modern art to America.

In each case the class is given an hour and a quarter instruction session before they undertake the research. The session is structured to first present a theoretical search strategy and a picture of the types of reference resources which exist in every subject area. Then we go on to deal with the specific tools which will be needed for the assignment. Most often students are given a written handout listing the sources which they will be using while the bulk of the class time is devoted to integrating that list within the theoretical framework.

So, yes, I do believe that we should be teaching students the details of doing research. We should be doing it because the research experience is beneficial on several levels, and we should be doing it through the use of imaginative, well structured research topics which students will find interesting as well as challenging.

I would like to close with a story about a young man at John Jay who, because of the need to repeat his first semester basic English course, had sat through at least two basic library instruction sessions, and had become, either because of that fact, or in spite of it, a regular library user. He came to me one day and said "Everytime I have come to you with a research question, you've been able to show me a good place to look. Can you help me now?" I naturally said, "I hope so," and he replied, "Do you have a book with a list of stupid questions?" It turned out that his assignment involved an analysis of poorly worded questions. Now that's a person who has learned to think in terms of libraries.

WILL THIS INNOVATION, LIBRARY INSTRUCTION, BE ADOPTED, BY AND BY?

Wayne Meyer

LOEX conferences reflect the state of the library instruction movement. This particular conference, the tenth, seems in part to have a new tone and emphasis to it, one of critical introspection and reevaluation. Instead of focusing on how to start or how to improve and expand a library instruction program, at this conference and with this panel this evening we are hearing some of our cherished assumptions and beliefs challenged or at least critically reviewed. These could be signs of maturation, and I myself think it's good to re--assess where we are now and to cast a cold, shrewd eye on where and how we aim to proceed in the 1980's.

During the next few minutes I want to make sure that one assumption is challenged (that perhaps some of you might still share), namely, that our particular educational innovation, called library, or bibliographic, instruction, will somehow become fully accepted and institutionalized because of its own intrinsic worth, because of the need for it and the success with it that we have seen and been convinced of (whether or not we could document this need and success with hard data). If, during the days when we were just exploring and getting started on our programs, we had had the time and energy and unusual foresight to soberly consider how an innovation can become fully adopted in an organization -- and I think it's understandable that most of us did not -- we no doubt would have suspected that it's a tricky, difficult question. But now the time has come, and I propose to take a very quick look at this matter of the adoption of innovations as applied to library instruction. I mean to show that there are ample causes for pessimism always, it seems, combined with some signs of hope. The next decade could indeed be decisive.

For my purpose this evening I'm going to adapt a three-part framework or three interweaving themes useful for examining the problems of organizational change, which are set forth by J. Victor Baldridge in an essay called "Organizational Change: Institutional Sagas, External Challenges, and Internal Politics." The three themes are 1) the underlying philosophy of a profession such as librarianship which forms the "content" of change, 2) the environment, which accounts for the "sources of change impetuses," and 3) politics, or the "processes" by which change is implemented.[1]

In regard, first, to the current underlying philosophy of academic librarianship or the deeply held values and beliefs about our missions and goals, we have some evidence of definite progress and hope. The fact is, I think, that the instruction of users is today assumed by librarians to be a legitimate, integral part of academic library services more than it was five or ten years ago and -- a few long past adumbrations and prophetic precedents notwithstanding -- more than ever before. While there is still much evidence among both university and college librarians of the "university library syndrome" described by Evan Farber in 1974,[2] -- that is, the passion for acquiring large collections but interpreting them to users only rather passively -- I think that Mr. Farber would be glad to agree that things have improved somewhat since. There are many, I know, who will argue that among the more senior and high-ranking librarians, who are also those who primarily give public articulation of our professional philosophy and also set or approve budgets and priorities, there is not

60

the same degree of commitment to library instruction as among all academic librarians, but I myself am not sure. It is interesting to note, for example, that instruction librarians in college libraries recently surveyed by Jon Lindgren indicated generally a high level of commitment to library instruction by their libraries' administrators, while in the same survey they indicated that the "total library profession's" commitment was distinctly lower and, in their judgment, still inadequate.[3] In all the ranks of librarians, many remain to be won over.

The second part of our framework for viewing organizational change, the environment, is more immediately crucial for us. The first part, the philosophy of a profession such as librarianship, is almost by definition slow to change and functions as a source of stability (or rigidity, depending upon your particular perspective), and, more important, is actually more or less reflexive *in response to* change. Whereas forces from the outside of an organization to a large degree provide the real motive power for initiating and supporting change. As Baldridge says, "many theorists have concluded that the prime impetus for large-scale change in organizations comes from external forces." And to preview the third part of our framework, namely, internal politics, Baldridge calls this emphasis on the environment "an interesting shift in perspective since most change-oriented literature examines small-scale human relations problems within an organization."[4]

For me, some of the most interesting current observations of the state of library instruction call attention to this crucial factor of the environment. As John Lubans says, we librarians "must change attitudes and policies of politicians and educators (including librarians), school boards and state boards of education."[5] Again, Jon Lindgren heavily stresses our present lack of "a useful, working tradition" and "broad cultural support" for instruction in library skills -- as contrasted to instruction in communication skills, for example -- and calls upon us to carefully shape a "rhetoric" in order to garner this broad cultural support.[6] However, no one seems to offer very comprehensive, detailed instructions on exactly how to change attitudes and build support on the outside. Furthermore, it will certainly prove difficult to differentiate between a) what is external and environmental in the sense of non-manipulable by librarians and b) our carefully controllable responses to external forces and influences. But there are some encouraging indicators. Carla Stoffle points to Library Leadership Conferences at the University of Wisconsin--Parkside which bring university administrators together with library administrators and instruction librarians as an example of a way to "provide support systems and greater acceptance for instruction programs across the country."[7] Also, the ACRL

Bibliographic Instruction Section's first steps toward establishing liaison with other, discipline-oriented associations might someday lead to a basis not just for winning over individual faculty members but for a useful tradition and ongoing broad support for library instruction in those other discipline-oriented associations.[8]

Let me just mention a few other major environmental factors which could help or hinder us in the years ahead. Retrenchment and fiscal stringency in higher education and libraries could help us argue logically for instruction in the intensive use of libraries in the absence of comprehensive collecting by libraries, or it could just discourage the adoption of innovative programs generally not to mention the growth of new programs. The new emphasis on teaching essential skills and academic competencies could help us, if library skills are recognized and promoted as among those essential skills. New technology in libraries could lead to a climate generally favorable to change and could lead to the recognition of new needs for teaching users to effectively cope with and exploit new library technology, or it could turn the emphasis in librarianship back toward exclusively technical services concerns.

The last part of our framework for viewing the problems of organizational change is politics. Politics, or the processes of implementing change, has received most of the attention in the abundant research and writing done by social scientists studying innovation and also in the few instances of librarians trying to come to grips with this issue. This research takes a human relations approach and studies the individual characteristics and interactions of change agents and the potential adopters of innovation, and often, it seems, the organizational settings and organizational factors are rather overlooked. Two years ago at this conference Larry Hardesty, using Everett M. Rogers' *The Communication of Innovation* and similar works as his sources, gave us some good advice primarily on how to win over individual faculty to cooperation in library instruction.[9] But as Baldridge and Deal say in their essay on "Change Processes in Educational Organizations," "Rogers' monumental study of innovation summarized the conclusions of the research in fifty-two major propositions, not one of which referred to a complex organization as the innovation adopter or to organizational features as affecting the process." Thus, the authors say, "the literature on innovation provides little help" even for those in a position and with a mind to try to bring about organizational change.[10]

But here, too, there are some signs of hope in library land. First is the trend toward participative management which has been pointed to as the particular managerial style most conducive to establishing the "teaching library."[11] In order for change to work out, certainly it helps if those who will carry it out are fully involved in planning it. Which brings us to the related technique of the self-study. After reviewing the programs involving library instruction that have been supported by the Council on Library Resources -- those programs that have directly or indirectly benefited so many of us here -- Nancy Gwinn concludes by saying that "it is time for a new approach" and points to the Council's support of Academic Library Programs, a form of self-study operated by the ARL Office of Management Studies, as their next step in strengthening academic libraries and their role in the educational process.[12]

It seems, finally, that if our innovation, called library instruction, is to be fully adopted in the 1980's, some of our emphasis will have to change. Some of our simple enthusiasm, zeal, and missionary spirit will have to give way a little more to perseverance, managerial shrewdness, and organizational skill.

NOTES

1. J. Victor Baldridge, "Organizational Change: Institutional Sagas, External Challenges, and Internal Politics," in *Governing Academic Organizations: New Problems, New Perspectives*, ed. by Gary L. Riley and J. Victor Baldridge (Berkeley: McCutchan Pub. Corp., 1977), pp. 123–144. The notion of an underlying philosophy of a profession is my rather free adaptation of the "organizational saga theme" used by Baldridge, that is, the "content of an institution's missions and goals. What does the institution believe in; what are its major guidelines; in what directions is it moving?" (p. 124). The commonality, I'd argue, is in how a group of people, within a particular institution or a particular profession, think collectively about themselves.

2. Evan Ira Farber, "College Librarians and the University Library Syndrome," in *The Academic Library: Essays in Honor of Guy R. Lyle*, ed. by Evan Ira Farber and Ruth Walling (Metuchen, NJ: Scarecrow Press, 1974), pp. 12--23.

3. Jon Lindgren, "Seeking a Useful Tradition for Library User Instruction in the College Library," in *Progress in Educating the Library User*, ed. by John Lubans, Jr. (New York: R.R. Bowker, 1978), p. 86, 89.

4. Baldridge, p. 124.

5. John Lubans, Jr., "Introduction: Seeking a Partnership between the Teacher and the Librarian," in *Progress in Educating the Library User*, p. 3.

6. Lindgren, p. 74, pp. 77–78.

7. Carla J. Stoffle in "Library Instruction: A Column of Opinion," ed. by Carolyn Kirkendall, *Journal of Academic Librarianship* 6 (March 1980): 41.

8. See Anne K. Beaubien, *Bibliographic Instruction within Library and Discipline Associations: A Survey of Contact Persons and Committees* (Chicago: ACRL, 1979). ERIC document ED 175 468.

9. Larry Hardesty, "Instructional Development in Library Use Education," in *Improving Library Instruction – How to Teach and How to Evaluate: Papers Presented at the Eighth Annual Conference on Library Orientation for Academic Libraries*, Eastern Michigan University, May 4–5, 1978 (Ann Arbor, MI: Pierian Press, 1979), pp. 11–35. Another relevant example is Anne Roberts, "The Politics of Library Instruction: Internal and External" (unpublished), a talk given at the College of Charleston, South Carolina, on March 23, 1979, at the Second Annual Conference on "Approaches to Bibliographic Instruction: Library Instruction in the Academic Curriculum." The presentation deals largely with the personality traits of instruction librarians, traits such as "intensity and fervor" and a "sense of mission" which make them successful innovators but which also result, says Roberts, in problems of resentment by and conflict with their librarian peers.

10. J. Victor Baldridge and Terrence E. Deal, "Change Processes in Educational Organizations," in *Governing Academic Organizations: New Problems, New Perspectives,* p. 82.

11. Patricia Senn Breivik, "Leadership, Management, and the Teaching Library," *Library Journal* 103 (October 15, 1978): 2048.

12. Nancy E. Gwinn, "Academic Libraries and Undergraduate Education: The CLR Experience," *College and Research Libraries* 41 (January 1980): 10–11.

THERE IS NO REAL NEED FOR STUDENTS
TO KNOW HOW TO USE THE LIBRARY

Roger Sween

Our overall goal as librarians is to maximize every person's awareness of and access to the materials and information they want and need. Three major methods of maximization present themselves: service, education, and public relations. Our special concern of educating the users we encounter or can corral promises to vastly enlarge upon the limited utilization of library resources that most people evidence. However, I am sorry to report that these excellent intentions are beside the point. For in actuality, there is no real need for students to know how to use the library.

We enter the library field, I believe, much as I did: full of theory, idealism, and enthusiasm, convinced of the central role of the library in learning, believing that information is the essential need of human beings, committed to doing our best to make the pursuit of information a lifelong process.

My education set me in the train of believing that all people were pining for more and more library service. At college it was difficult to find a seat in the library unless you came early; you saved a place by carrying two coats – an outer coat which you wore to make Minnesota weather passable and an inner sweater or jacket which you placed over the chair, giving every appearance that you had just pushed back from the table and were off somewhere, looking something up. Certainly the high school students, teachers, and later the university students and faculty I would encounter would demonstrate this same constant, insatiable thirst for information.

A one-person school library proved to be a busy place, but I began to get suspicious. In a small school of 300, I came to know everyone, but after a month I realized it was the poorest students, academically speaking, that I had come to know first. Other teachers would come to the library, saying in surprise, "What is Johnny Trouble doing here?" Well, these and other regulars found the library a more relaxed place than the many monitored study halls they had during the week. They came every day and flipped through magazine after magazine. My suspicions markedly increased when a year later in a second high school, also rural but in a different part of the state, I witnessed the induction of a new crop of National Honor Society students. To my surprise as I looked over the list of twenty students, I found that none of them was a regular library user. Such an opportunity could not pass: When surveyed they each reported they were too busy to use the high school library. Classes, band and

65

chorus, and extra-curricular activities after school took all their time. They used the public library, they said, when they had research to do.

My skepticism peaked early in my university career. A graduate student needed to work on a certain topic which clearly necessitated the use of *Psychological Abstracts*, and the student was uninitiated. Perhaps because this person was a graduate student, and an older adult, and set upon a clearly defined research topic, I felt it was necessary to give a full explanation of *Psych Abstracts*. So I went into the full rundown on how the indexes had to be consulted, the abstract numbers followed up in the monthly issues, how the citations had to be deciphered, distinguishing between the monographs and the serials, and between the periodicals and the other cataloged serials, how reference had to be made to the card catalog and to the periodicals list, how keeping track of one's search process was expected if interlibrary loan followup should be needed or desired, and other necessary procedures -- all this in the days before widespread online searching. The student looked and me and replied very calmly, I'm sure, "Isn't there an easier way to do this?"

Doubtless, I responded, probably with some alternative bibliographic search scenario; I don't recall exactly. I next saw this student again at graduation, walking across the platform to receive the master's degree, bearing the regalia, showing honors had been received. And I wondered, was this how honors were earned, doing the easy thing, finding the easier way? And I noted with increasing horror that among all the honors graduates that day, among the graduates at large, were many whom I had never seen before. How could this be? In those days I worked at least twenty scheduled hours per week at the Reference Desk; and, due to a lack of space, my own desk was right in the reading room and reference collection. Why had I never seen these students? How could they escape the institution without my having had some contact with them?

Knowing that our own observation abilities are limited, that they are clouded by our own prejudices and habits and mindsets, it is possible to counter the conclusions we find ourselves driven to by seeking other observations. However, when librarians get together at lunch from work or at conferences and start to unload on one another, the reinforcement of one's own beliefs comes swiftly. The tale of woe spreads; no one is using us the way we think we ought to be used.

Turn to the literature of library instruction. It's impressive that so many have worked so industriously and imaginatively over a very long period of time. Read a little and you get refueled to do more and better. And there have been some accounts that give every indication of having won the day at certain campuses and with large numbers of faculty. But, sadly, the followup research is a dismal blank. We cannot show that library instruction, or, library service either, have any effect on or relation to future academic success. Indeed, it is easy to suspect that the minority of students who are at our shoulders all the time, who are constantly reading, inquiring, seeking for answers and understanding, that they may do poorer, as measured by the grading system, than do the drudges, who docilely and dutifully have turned themselves into what Daniel Fader has called "right answer machines."

As a framework of how the whole question of library utilization might be judged, a model can be posed as to the kind of demand on a library that could be expected in an academic institution. Consider this as a minimum: How many times a week does a question occur to a person that cannot be answered by one's own resources or those that are immediately available? How many times a week would you expect, as a minimum, that a student who is taking four to six courses, subjects that are covering new ground, would encounter some problem which would channel this learner into the library for assistance? Be conscious of and keep track of your own questions, your own need for information, and you will soon discover that from work, that arising in conversation, that in following the current press of events, numerous questions occur in a week which we cannot readily answer, which we ought to follow up in the library.

Posit then that at a minimum, a bare minimum, you might expect such a question to occur at least once a week to each student. Multiply this single question by the number of students who are enrolled. Divide this product of total weekly questions by the number of hours of reference service available. This resulting quotient of anticipated questions per hour should then predict the amount of staff that you need to have available to answer the flood at your desk. Five thousand students, the number of students at UW–Platteville when I first envisioned this model, ought to generate 5,000 questions per week. Open 80 hours a week, we could expect 62.5 questions per hour on the average. Observing that when you are working full tilt you can answer twelve to fifteen questions per hour, such a volume of questions would require four or five people at the desk just to stave off the thundering hordes of information starved students who are constantly camped at your door.

Obviously, we don't even experience what can be considered the smallest minimum of possible demand. All studies of library use show that in all types of libraries in all places over several years, it is always a minority, a fraction of a fraction, that makes consistent and regular use of the library. Even in education settings, use is poor, and the use that does exist falls off with graduation. We discover high school and college graduates who never read a book again.

Now hope springs eternal, and the desire to do what we have seen that we ought to do propels us to find explanations and thereby solutions for problems that we can identify. Realizing that we have not been in a position to actually generate the demand upon the library, that we must rely upon the classroom teacher to drive the student to us, makes us examine what goes on in the classroom.

In the classroom the teacher is one of the truly independent autocrats left in the world. Teachers are earnestly interested in their students' learning, but it is basically learning limited to what the teacher knows and the textbook provides. Children are not free to get up and go to other sources at the moment a question occurs; that would be too disruptive. Teachers are in possession of the truth, and we avoid the plague that could attack every dictum: "Is this really so?" "How do we know?" "Where can we find out for sure?" The information skill that is most consistently and successfully learned in the entire educational process is how to suppress questions. "Oh, that is not important." "We've no time for that now." "It's too much work to find the answer." "Will this be on the test?"

Beyond the classroom there exists a societal bias for the instant information the television set provides, for the quick digest of everything into a functional format; there exists the desire for immediate gratification, including answers without seeking for information. We witness the penchant of politicians to survey their constituents to find out what they think on the issues and the spectacle of citizens telephoning the President to ask him questions that the last four issues of a news magazine could settle.

At base, information is not valued. Why did it take years to get a recalcitrant President to call a White House Conference on Libraries and Information Services? And why did it take added months to move a partisan Congress to appropriate money? Certainly not because libraries are political, controversial, or expensive. When the various Governor's conferences and the White House Conference met, they were under a pall of silence. In my state the Governor's budget request for the current biennium calls for almost three times the funding to fight Dutch Elm disease as it does for the entire budget of the Office of Public Libraries and Interlibrary Cooperation.

When you are committed to the pursuit of information, you begin to see all issues in terms of the way in which information is used. The President, whose position is primarily to make decisions on the information processing in his purview, is challenged by his rivals on all sides to stop that legitimate activity, which they denigrate as "rose garden campaigning," to join in the unilluminating rhetoric. Managers of large corporations, whose jobs are to use information in decision making, and who are paid six-figure salaries for their judgment, are not expected to make consistently right decisions, only on balance more right than wrong decisions. Failing even that majority, they can appeal for federal bailouts to guarantee the non-pursuit of information. We find ourselves unable to escape the inflation spiral because inflation is the only way that has been found to uniformly spread the results of failing to seek and accept the measures by which the economy must operate.

What can be done to increase the recognition of the value of information and thereby its use? As a basis we need to know the process which people go through in determining whether or not they are going to pursue information. When we have unravelled that psychology, we can begin to structure better how we should make the decision more operative. In the meantime, let us all agree as professionals in the information field what it is that people ought to know as a basis for seeking information so that we can join forces to develop these skills and competencies with mutual knowledge and sequential accumulation.

I have stressed that library literacy is not needed; I believe this to be the current worsening state. And I don't see that when we have more information and better ways of retrieving it and more potential demand for information that people will be any better at going about getting it. But that doesn't mean that I don't think they ought to be. You don't need to know how to use the library: You can get through high school and college without darkening the door, you can succeed in business and live out your lives without a library consciousness. But you cannot realize your full human potential without one. For although there is no real need for information seeking skills, there is still a metaphysical one.

USER EDUCATION EVALUATION

Nancy Fjällbrant
Chalmers University of Technology

In this paper, I plan to examine the need for, and purpose of, evaluation in library user education. Evaluation will be considered in relation to four parameters: targets, scope, methods and timing. Examples of different kinds of evaluation will be described in relation to these parameters.

I. *The role of the academic library*

The traditional role of the university library was that of a *store* of precious material – manuscripts and books. With the invention of Gutenberg's moveable type printing, which led to the production of multi-copy editions, and the spread of higher education, the *service* function was added to the warehouse role. Service was facilitated by the provision of such tools as union catalogues of book and periodical holdings, and abstracts and indexes. Library resources were provided for inter-library lending and reader services departments. The aim is to provide an efficient information service for all who ask to use it. In recent years, many libraries have an additional major role – that of *active exploitation*. Whereas in the service library, service is provided for all those users who request to use the available information resources, in the active exploitation library, an attempt is made to inform *potential users* about the information resources and services available in the library. This role is of increasing importance with the development of computerized information retrieval services. User orientation and education play an important part in the process of active exploitation of library resources and the last fifteen years have seen a considerable growth and development in this field of librarianship.

II. *The need for evaluation*

The development of a new function raises questions about the allocation of staff and financial resources. User education is often regarded by librarians as an independent (and luxury?) function, which can be conveniently reduced in times of economic difficulty. Against this background, there is a need to evaluate user education programmes, in order to obtain information which can be used for planning and the allocation of funds and staff within the library. The *purpose of evaluation* has been described by Astin and Panos in the following words -- "the fundamental purpose of evaluation is to produce information that can be used in educational decision making." (Astin and Panos, 1971.) "Educational decisions (like other administrative decisions) involve choices between available alternatives which are based on both educational and economic factors, and which often involve subjective judgment and value decision." (Fjällbrant and Stevenson, 1978.) The purpose of evaluation is to provide information which is useful for making rational decisions, such as in the allocation of staff and financial resources. Evaluation can be used to provide information about the effects of a user education programme, about the functioning of one particular course, about needs for modification in existing programmes, about the effectiveness of various teaching methods in achieving a pre-specified goal, or about the adoption of an innovation. Evaluation should form an essential part of any programme of library orientation or instruction. Lubans pointed out that "the results of evaluation not only present alternatives for better programmes but should also provide standards of performance for such instruction." (Lubans, 1972.) More and more librarians are becoming aware of the need to evaluate user education -- as Galvin expressed this, "There is a consistent recognition . . . that user education programmes ought to be conducted in a climate of rigorous evaluation and accountability." (Galvin, 1978.)

III. *The parameters of evaluation*

Evaluation can be regarded from a number of different angles and directed towards different aspects of the educational course or programme. In order to evaluate, it is necessary to formulate goals and objectives. Yet, as pointed out by Young and Brennan, "many programs of instruction are designed and implemented without identifiable objectives." (Young and Brennan, 1978.) Surveys on library and bibliographic instruction in southeastern academic libraries and in libraries in Pennsylvania revealed that only a small percent of the libraries had written statements of objectives and the majority did not evaluate their courses in user education (Ward, 1976 and Whildin, 1976.) A survey on user education programmes in Swedish academic libraries showed that, while there had been an increase in the number of libraries attempting to evaluate their educational programmes since 1973, the majority still did not carry out any evaluation (Fjällbrant, 1977). Two examples of evaluation based on a statement of aims and objectives are to be seen in the British SCONUL tape/slide evaluation project (Hills, Lincoln and Turner, 1977), and in the Travelling Workshops Experiment (Harris, Clark and Douglas, 1978). Evaluation based on the achievement of pre-specified goals and objectives can be directed towards the educational process or product (targets). Evaluation can be described in terms of scope, methods used and timing.

III.1. *The targets of evaluation*

An educational course or programme consists of an educational *process* (learning/teaching situation, methods, media) and an educational *product* (sum of total individual output in relation to pre-specified goals). The relationship between the educational process and product is illustrated in Figure 1, where S = student input in terms of pre-knowledge.

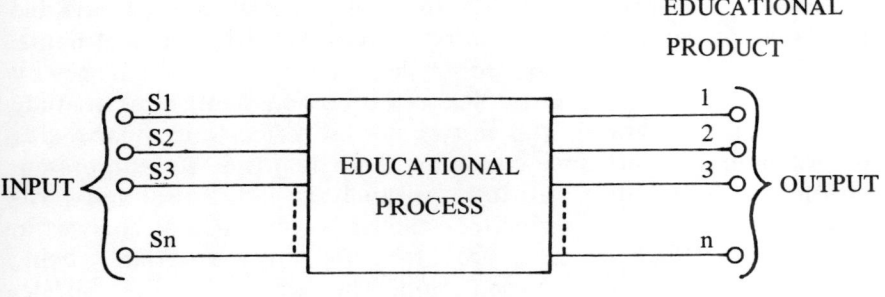

Figure 1: Relationship between educational process and product.

Evaluation may be directed towards the educational process in a given course or programme or towards the output or educational product.

III.2. *The scope of evaluation*

Evaluation may be carried out on individual courses, educational programmes or a general educational system. Evaluation can also be carried out on specific media -- workbooks, tape/slide programmes, self-instructional learning packages, etc. It is useful to make a distinction between assessment and evaluation: *Individual assessment* is concerned with the specific achievement of the individual student, with regard either to his/her contemporary student group, or to pre-specified goals; *Evaluation* is concerned with the effects of a given educational course, programme or system. Fjällbrant pointed out that "many of the evaluation studies described in the library literature give accounts of the evaluation of specific methods and media rather than evaluation of programmes of instruction." (Fjällbrant, 1976.)

III.3. *The methods of evaluation*

Evaluation can be classified according to the method used. Three main types of evaluation can be described:
The psychometric
The sociological or management
The illuminative or responsive

III.3.1 *Psychometric evaluation*

Psychometric evaluation has evolved from the psychological discipline. In this type of evaluation, it is assumed that it is possible to expose experimental and control groups to different treatments, while all other variables are controlled, and to measure changes by means of achievement tests. These are complemented by attitude questionnaires. Thus in the testing of the effects of a tape/slide programme, students are given a pre-test, then they see the presentation and complete a post-test. An analysis of the pre- and post-tests is carried out, in order to establish any significant changes in performance; such changes are attributed to the variable being studied -- the tape/slide presentation. The assumption that "irrelevant" variables can be controlled is, in many cases, completely unjustifiable.

III.3.2. *Sociological or management evaluation*

The management or sociological approach to evaluation has developed from the discipline of industrial sociology. This method is concerned with changes in the structure or use of an organization or the roles of participants in the educational programme. Use is made of interviews and questionnaires. Attention is focused on the organization undergoing change, rather than on comparisons with a control group.

III.3.3. *Illuminative or responsive evaluation*

The third type of evaluation is based on the use of participant observation and interviews as a means to obtain an overall view of an educational course or programme. This type of evaluation has been called "illuminative" observation (Parlett and Hamilton, 1972) and "responsive" evaluation (Stake, 1974). Illuminative evaluation is not limited by the initial formulation of aims, but allows for the finding of "unexpected" results. Research is focused on what is actually happening in response to an innovation. Illuminative evaluation is concerned, not so much with testing an educational course, as with describing and understanding the way in which it works and the reactions of the teachers and students participating in it. Observational studies and explorative interviews are often used to obtain this information. Questionnaires and achievement scores may be used but they are rarely given high priority. This type of evaluation is very time-consuming and therefore expensive. A further disadvantage is the difficulty of being objective to the findings.

III.4. *The timing of evaluation*

Evaluation can be carried out at different times with regard to the development of a course or programme. Scriven distinguished between two types of evaluation -- formative and summative. *Formative evaluation* is carried out early, during the development of a course. It aims to provide feedback about the functioning of the different parts of the course -- information which can provide a basis for modification of the educational process. *Summative evaluation* is concerned with the evaluation of the product of the course or programme. It is carried out relatively late and provides information about the overall worth of a course.

IV. *Examples of evaluation of user education at Chalmers University Library, Gothenburg*

IV.1. *Evaluation of MEDIATRON online orientation programmes*

During the last decade there has been a rapid growth in the availability of computerized information retrieval. Chalmers Library has an extensive user education programme with courses/training for over 2,000 people per year. In connection with this programme, it was necessary to produce inexpensive and reliable teaching material for orientation in online information retrieval. The objectives for an orientation programme were defined. A number of multi-media programmes, using the MEDIATRON teaching aid developed by

Vickery and Pratt (Pratt and Vickery, 1977) were made. The ME-DIATRON is a modified tape recorder, which is designed to carry out simultaneous recording of audio-commentaries, trigger pulses for photographic slides, and digital signals from a computerized information retrieval system. Figure 2 shows the MEDIATRON demonstration configuration. Orientation programmes were made, showing searches on:

a) The use of wind energy for heating (Swedish version 11 minutes, English version 12 minutes).

b) The presence of DDT in seals in the Baltic (Swedish version 14 minutes, English version 13 minutes).

c) Home-Care for geriatric patients (Swedish version 18 minutes).

These orientation programmes were evaluated for use with different groups: undergraduate and postgraduate engineering students, and library school students. Evaluation was carried out by means of pre- and post-tests designed to measure the "immediate learning effect," and by means of a detailed questionnaire on attitudes to this type of learning programme and to the presentation itself. (For a detailed description of this evaluation see Fjällbrant and Hard, 1979). The pre- and post-tests showed that for all the groups there was a good immediate learning effect -- with one exception -- the names of the information systems. Details of how the information retrieval was carried out, where it was available and what kind of result could be expected were learnt easily by exposure to the short orientation programme.

The attitude studies showed that all the groups of students had enjoyed the presentation, found the contents interesting and thought that this was a good method for teaching about online information retrieval. The library school students were particularly positive about this type of instruction -- 64% (very good method) and 36% (good method) as compared with 16% (very good), 66% (good) -- undergraduates, and 33% (very good), 57% (good) for the post-graduates.

These evaluation studies are an example of psychometric evaluation, directed towards a specific type of teaching presentation (part of the process). The results obtained showed that the multi-media MEDIATRON programmes developed at Chalmers could be used successfully for orientation and promotion of online information retrieval. As a result of the evaluation, further programmes have been developed, and a research project started on the use of BYGGDOK -- a nordic database with building and town planning information -- for students of civil engineering.

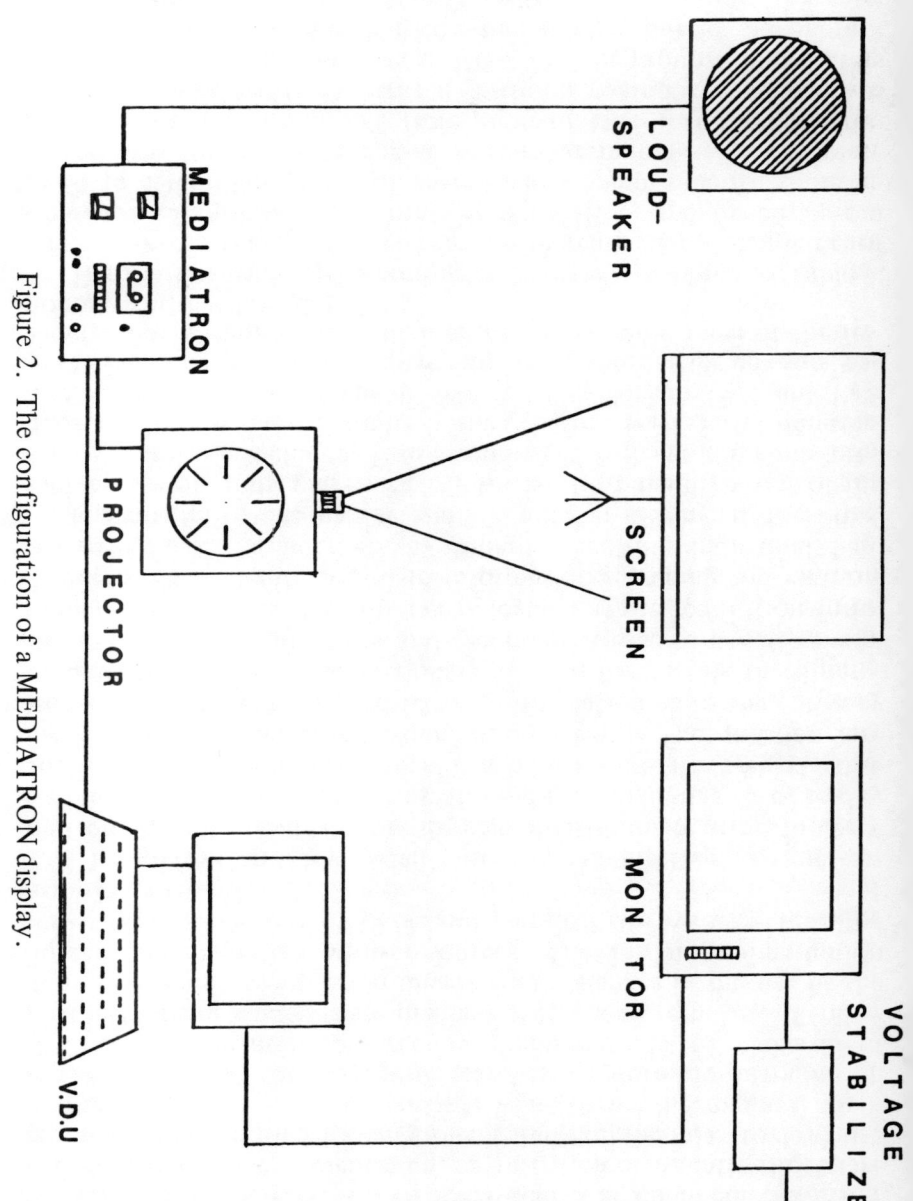

Figure 2. The configuration of a MEDIATRON display.

IV.2. *Evaluation of a programme of user education by means of a long-term study of the patterns of library use*

Prior to 1974, very few of the students at Chalmers University had received library orientation or instruction. Against this background, it was decided to carry out a study on the "day-to-day" use of the library -- the reasons people went there, the material used, success in carrying out literature searches -- before the introduction of the user education programme (Fjällbrant, 1976). Subsequent post-instruction studies were planned over a long term period (minimum six years), in order to measure any changes in the use of the library and its information resources. The initial pre-instruction survey was carried out in 1974, and identical surveys were repeated in 1975 and 1979.

The surveys on "day-to-day" use of Chalmers Library were carried out by means of a short six page questionnaire given to every user entering the library during three days -- Tuesday, Wednesday and Thursday -- mid--week days of a typical mid-term week (avoiding beginning of term and examiration weeks). The questionnaire (see Appendix) was designed to give information as to the category of user, the primary and secondary reasons for visiting the library, the materials used primarily and secondarily, ease of use of general library tools such as the subject catalogue and the requisition form, degree of success with regard to information searching and material obtained, and the number of students receiving individual help from members of the library staff. A number of general questions, such as use of study places, and views on the general lay-out of the library were also included. Users were asked to leave the completed questionnaire at the distribution table before leaving the building. The response rate was high -- 98% in 1974, 96% in 1975 and 95% in 1979. The completed questionnaires were analyzed and the average day response was obtained by taking an average of the responses over the three days.

Distribution of users according to category is shown in Table I. Table I shows that there has been an increase in the daily use of Chalmers Library by 17% from 1974 to 1975, and by 56% from 1974 to 1979. The group of users mainly responsible for these increases was the Chalmers engineering undergraduates (25% increase from 1974 to 1975 and 53% from 1974 to 1979). The undergraduate course in information retrieval (14 hours compulsory course) was introduced in the academic year 1974/75. The group "other" users included secretaries, members of the general public and library school students. The 1979 survey showed a high figure for this category due to a study visit of trainee research librarians from the Swedish College of Librarianship, during the week of the survey.

Table I. Daily users of Chalmers Library.

User Category	Numbers per day		
	1974	1975	1979
Undergraduate (Chalmers)	147	185	225
Postgraduate	22	24	31
Academic staff	6	7	8
Industrial employee	12	8	11
Undergraduate (Gothenburg University)	19	17	25
High school pupil	4	2	9
"Other"	14	13	30
Refusals	4	11	19
Total	228	267	355

The primary and secondary reasons for use of Chalmers Library were examined, and these have been added together and shown in Table II.

Table II shows that whereas the number of students using the library for reading "set" course work remained fairly constant during the five year period, there were increases in the use of the library for literature searching and for reading non-course material. The increase in the amount of photocopying is due to the increasing availability of copying machines from 1978 onwards (periodicals may not be borrowed). A visit to the library cafe was often the secondary reason for a visit to the library. Other reasons for use were "use of the telex apparatus," "writing up laboratory notes," "work on a group project," "working on mathematical exercises," etc.

In a similar way, the sum of the material and media used each day (firstly and secondly) is shown in Table III.

Table III shows increases in the use of periodicals, abstracts/indexes, and reference literature -- dictionaries, handbooks, tables. Micromedia were not used to any extent, nor were doctoral dissertations.

Table II. Primary and secondary reasons for use of Chalmers Library.

Reason for use	Numbers per day		
	1974	1975	1979
Read "set" literature	102	104	119
Read other literature	35	46	72
Borrow literature	19	23	36
Return material	27	24	17
Literature search	49	80	88
Photocopying	6	4	50
Essay writing	7	9	11
Social reasons	9	10	31
Visit the cafe	42	54	63
Do something else	29	30	48

Table III. What is used?

Material used	Numbers per day		
	1974	1975	1979
Journals/periodicals	60	67	100
"Course" literature	60	65	78
Books (other than course lit)	18	21	39
Abstracts/indexes	14	39	75
Reference literature	12	20	45
Microfiche/microfilm	0	0	1
Dissertations	1	1	1
Popular magazines	12	9	13
Something else	10	14	20
Own materials	94	87	100

The use of various library tools was also examined, and the findings for the three years are shown in Table IV.

Table IV shows a considerable increase in the use of IR-tools such as abstracts, indexes and bibliographies. The use of Chalmers list of periodicals has also increased, whereas the use of the alphabetic catalogue showed first an increase then a decrease. This may be due to the "opening" of the stacks in 1978.

Table IV. Use of library tools

Library tool	Numbers per day		
	1974	1975	1979
Alphabetic catalogue	22	40	24
Subject catalogue	14	28	26
Chalmers periodicals list	18	27	42
Information retrieval tools	12	35	82

In 1974, 56% of the users obtained all or nearly all of the books that they wanted to borrow or look at, the corresponding figure for 1975 was 61% and for 1979, 40%. For periodicals the figures were: 1974 – 76%, 1975 – 73%, and 1979 – 88%. These figures may reflect the literature selection policy of the library (85% of the literature allowance is used for periodicals, and 1978 was a year with lack of new monographs).

Already one year after the introduction of the programme of user education at Chalmers Library, it was possible to see a change in the patterns of use of the library. These changes were to be seen in the changing patterns of behaviour of the engineering undergraduates, whereas other groups did not show these changes. The changes -- increased use of the library for such tasks as information retrieval and a wider use of non-set material -- continued in 1979. Change has also occurred in the behavior of the postgraduate group in the 1979 survey. The library had become a place to be used by students, or as one industrial engineer put it, "the greatest change in the library in the last ten years is that there are lots of students there now."

This long term study of changing patterns of use in a library is an example of the use of the sociological or management type of evaluation being used for a summative evaluation of the products of an educational programme. The information obtained has been used as the basis for planning and negotiations in connection with the budget of the library.

IV.3. *Illuminative evaluation of a course in information retrieval for undergraduate engineering students*

A 14-hour course in information retrieval was introduced in 1974, at Chalmers Library, for some 800 engineering students per year. This course was evaluated in a number of ways, one of which was by illuminative evaluation. This was carried out by means of detailed observations on the behavior of the students and teachers during actual courses and by a series of open-ended interviews with course participants. This was a form of non-preordinate evaluation, in which it was possible to find unexpected information.

One unexpected finding that came out of the interviews with the students was their fear of going into and using a university library: Student: "So you come into the library and it's like a jungle, lots of books and so many of them in English." Another student said that one result of the course would be that the fear of going into a library would be reduced. Student: "Well, you know what I mean, one didn't want to try these things, because, well you'd heard that it was such a difficult business to borrow a book, so one tried to avoid it for as long as possible and borrowed books from the public library instead." Another student: "Well you can say that when we came here, we hadn't a clue about how to start, knew nothing, it was just like a jungle."

Another student said that he had visited the library previous to the course and tried to carry out a literature search. Student: "I didn't get anywhere at first." Interviewer: "What did you do?" Student: "First I came in and saw some books, then I found that they were really lists of things (abstracts and indexes). Then somebody helped me and I found a book. Then I went home and read the book." Interviewer: "Did you go to the Information Desk?" Student: "Yes. She helped me to find my book." Interviewer: "Just one book?" Student: "Well she looked in a card catalogue, and then I looked there." Interviewer: "Was it the Subject Catalogue?" Student: "Yes, subject something or other." Interviewer: "Didn't you borrow any more books?" Student: "No, it seemed so meaningless."

These interviews can serve to illustrate the fear and uncertainty that are experienced by student users in using a large academic library. This type of evaluation allows the evaluator to penetrate deeper than the surface and obtain information outside the rather narrow limits of the course goals and objectives. This particular study led to the development of a simple colour-shape coded sign system to help new users.

V. *Discussion*

In Section IV different examples of evaluation studies have been given. Any learning/teaching situation is complex and depends on a variety of factors, many of which are random and unpredictable. It is, therefore, desirable to make use of more than one method when trying to evaluate a given course or programme, in order to obtain as complete a picture as possible of the educational process and product being studied. Each method has its limitations; in many cases it is very difficult to carry out tests under truly controlled conditions. Detailed discussions and open-ended interviews provide valuable information, but they are time-consuming and therefore expensive. Any tests chosen must be relevant to the total situation.

The need for evaluation in library user orientation and instruction has long been recognized by librarians, but the practice of evaluation requires time, patience and adequate financial resources. Evaluation must be considered at the initial planning stage in courses of instruction and for new teaching media.

NOTES

Astin, A.W. & Panos, R.J., "The Evaluation of Education Programs," in R.L. Thorndike (ed.) *Educational Measurement*, 2d ed. Washington, 1971. pp. 733--751.

Fjällbrant, N. & Stevenson, M., *User Education in Libraries*. London: Bingley, 1978. 173pp.

Lubans, J., "Evaluating Library-User Education Programs," *Drexel Library Quarterly* 8 (1972) 3, p. 325.

Galvin, T.J., Foreword, in J. Lubans (ed.) *Progress in Educating the Library User*. New York: Bowker, 1978. 230pp.

Young, A.P. & Brennan, E.B., "Bibliographic Instruction: A Review of research and applications," in J. Lubans (ed.) *Progress in Educating the Library User*. New York: Bowker, 1978. pp. 13--28.

Ward, J.E., "Library and Bibliographic Instruction in Southeastern Academic Libraries," *Southeastern Librarian* 26 (1976). pp. 148--159.

Whildin, S.L., "Library Instruction in Pennsylvania Academic Libraries," *PLA Bulletin* 31 (1976) 8.

Fjällbrant, N., "User Education Programmes in Swedish Academic Libraries. A Study of Developments in the Years 1973–1977," *CTHB-Publikation* nr. 14. Göteborg: Chalmers University Library, 1977. 53 pp.

Hills, P.J., Lincoln, L. & Turner, L.P., *Evaluation of Tape/Slide Guides for Library Instruction*. British Library Research and Development Reports, no. 5378HC. London: British Library, 1977.

Harris, C., Clark, D., & Douglas, A., "The Travelling Workshops Experiment," in J. Lubans (ed.) *Progress in Educating the Library User*. New York: Bowker, 1978. pp. 171–181.

Fjällbrant, N., *The Development of a Programme of User Education at Chalmers University of Technology Library*. Ph.D. thesis. Guildford: University of Surrey, 1976. 439 pp.

Parlett, M. & Hamilton, D., "Evaluation as Illumination: A New Approach to the Study of Innovatory Programs," *Occasional Paper. Centre for Research in the Educational Sciences*. Edinburgh: University of Edinburgh, 1972.

Stake, R.E., "Program Evaluation, Particularly Responsive Evaluation," *Reports from the Institute of Education, University of Gothenburg* no. 35, Gothenburg, 1974.

Pratt, G. & Vickery, A., "The Development of Multi-Media Teaching Aids for Users of Computer-Based Information Retrieval Systems," *Program* 11 (1977) 1. pp. 10–15.

Fjällbrant, N. & Hard, S., "Design and Evaluation of Multimedia Programmes for Education in On–Line Information Retrieval," *Tidskrift for Dokumentation* 35 (1979) 5. pp. 101–106.

APPENDIX

CHALMERS UNIVERSITY LIBRARY
MAIN LIBRARY

STUDY OF LIBRARY USE

We need *your* help! Can you *spare a few minutes* to answer the following questions before you leave the library? Your answers can help us to improve our service. Please read the alternative answers for each question and circle the most appropriate answer. *Thank you for your help!*

1. I am:

Undergraduate	1
Postgraduate	2
Lecturer	3
Professor	4
Student (from high school)	5
Industrial employee	6
'Other'	7

   If 'other' please specify:

2. Which School of Engineering do you belong to?

E (Electrical)	1
M (Mechanical)	2
P (Physics)	3
C (Civil)	4
Ch (Chemical)	5
A (Architecture)	6
Question not applicable	0

3. How many terms (including the present one) have you studied at Chalmers:
   Question not applicable:

4. Age (in years):

5. *Today* I used Chalmers Main Library first and foremost for:

Reading set course material (Book, compendia, etc.)	1
Borrowing set course material	2
Reading non-set course material (Books, periodicals, etc.)	3
Borrowing non-set course material	4
Literature search for undergraduate thesis	5
Literature search in connection with a research project	6
'Literature-project'	7
Return material (Books, periodicals, etc.)	8
Photocopying of material	9
Essay or article writing	10
For social reasons – e.g. to meet friends	11
To visit the cafe	12
To do 'something else'	13

6. *Today* I used Chalmers Main Library for the secondary purpose of:
Reading set course material (Book, compendia, etc.) 1
Borrowing set course material 2
Reading non-set course material (Books, periodicals etc.) 3
Borrowing non-set course material 4
Literature search for undergraduate thesis 5
Literature search in connection with a research project 6
'Literature-project' 7
Return material (Books, periodicals, etc.) 8
Photocopying of material 9
Essay or article writing 10
For social reasons -- e.g. to meet friends 11
To visit the cafe 12
To do 'something else' 13
I had *no* 'secondary purpose'

7. *Today* I used, first and foremost:
Journals/periodicals 1
Set "course" material 2
Books (other than course literature) 3
Reference material (dictionaries. handbooks, encyclopedias 4
Bibliographic aids (indexes, abstracts etc.) 5
Theses 6
Microfilm or microfiche material 7
Recreational literature -- popular magazines 8
Something else 9
Nothing (for example brought own material) 0

8. *Today* I used as secondary material:
Journals/periodicals 1
Set "course" material 2
Books (other than course literature) 3
Reference material (dictionaries. handbooks, encyclopedias) 4
Bibliographic aids (indexes, abstracts etc.) 5
Theses 6
Microfilm or microfiche material 7
Recreational literature -- popular magazines 8
Something else 9
Nothing (for example brought own material) 0

9. *Today* I used:
The alphabetic author catalogue
(Card catalogue in reference hall)

10. Subject card catalogue.

11. *Today* I used:
    DK catalogue (abstract catalogue) in reference hall.
    List of journals.
    Bibliographic aids -- on the shelves in the reference hall.
    What do you think of the subject catalogue? Is it:

Very difficult to use	1
Difficult to use	2
Rather difficult to use	3
Rather easy to use	4
Easy to use	5
Don't use	0

12. *Today* my success with regard to literature searching was:

Very good (found everything)	1
Good (found nearly everything)	2
Rather good (found something)	3
Poor (found few items)	4
Very poor (found nothing)	5
Question non-applicable	0

13. *Today* I obtained, of the *books* I wanted to borrow:

Everything	1
Nearly everything	2
Something	3
Not much	4
Nothing	5
Question non-applicable	0

14. *Today* I obtained, of the *periodicals* I wanted to borrow:

Everything	1
Nearly everything	2
Something	3
Not much	4
Nothing	5
Question non-applicable	0

15. The library staff were *today*:

Very helpful	1
Helpful	2
Rather helpful	3
Not particularly helpful	4
Not helpful at all	5
Question non-applicable	0

16. Do you think the lay-out of Chalmers Main Library is:
Very good 1
Good 2
Rather good 3
Poor 4
Very poor 5

17. The reprocentre (for photocopies) is situated in the cellar. Do you think the position of the reprocentre is:
Very good 1
Good 2
Rather good 3
Poor 4
Very poor 5
Don't use 0

18. At Chalmers Main Library the main part of the literature is stored in a closed-access book-store. Do you think that open-access to literature would be:
Very desirable 1
Desirable 2
Hardly necessary 3
Unnecessary 4
No opinion 5

19. What do you think of the present loan-request form?
Very difficult to complete 1
Difficult to complete 2
Rather difficult to complete 3
Rather easy to complete 4
Easy to complete 5

20. Do you think that the hours of opening for Chalmers Main Library are adequate for your needs?
Yes 1
No 2

21. When you wish to work at Chalmers Main Library, do you find a place:
Always 1
Nearly always 2
Sometimes 3
Never 4
Don't work there 0

22. What is your *total impression* of Chalmers Main Library?

Very good	1
Good	2
Rather good	3
Poor	4
Very poor	5

Thank you!

LIBRARY SIGN SYSTEMS: AN INSTRUCTIONAL MEDIUM

John Kupersmith
University of Pennsylvania

Signs are among the most basic, and at the same time most indispensable, media available for library instruction.[1] While the idea of libraries using signs to communicate with their users is a familiar one, in practice this idea has often been applied in a haphazard and ineffective manner. In recent years, there has been a growing interest among librarians in exploiting the potential of a planned, systematic approach to displaying information in the library environment. The term "sign system," as used here, refers to the product of such planning -- a coordinated series of related components which work together to present information in a structured way and achieve specific objectives.

The current interest among librarians in informational graphics and sign systems is traceable to a number of trends both within and outside the profession. Over the past two decades, librarians have become more and more concerned with user behavior, with the interface between user and library, and consequently with various forms of library instruction. Problems of scale resulting from large user populations and limited budgets have led some librarians, particularly in university settings, to concentrate on media and methods that enable them to reach as many users as possible with basic library information. At the same time, designers have given increasing attention to the need for informational graphics in public buildings; both the professional practice of sign design and the technology available for sign construction have gained in sophistication. The confluence of these trends has led to a number of relevant conferences, to the publication of some useful literature, and even to official recognition in the form of a recently established Library of Congress subject heading for "Library signs." Although published information on the number and quality of actual library sign projects is scant, a recent survey by the Association of Research Libraries revealed that 37 of 68 responding libraries had developed sign systems.[2]

Like other media employed in library instruction, sign systems derive their importance from the needs that library users experience as they search for information. While users derive considerable knowledge and essential skills from the activities that are collectively known as "bibliographic instruction," their experience of the library extends beyond these structured activities. Users experience the library from day to day as a facility, as a medium through which they must move to reach the information and materials they seek, and as a source of informational cues to guide them in this process. Users will look for and receive cues from the environment whether these cues are planned or unplanned, consistent or random, helpful or confusing. Whether the environment will be an aid or an obstacle to the user depends on the extent to which the library acts to shape its environment as an instructional tool.

Actual signing practices in libraries vary widely. In the most extreme cases, the effect of nonexistent or minimal signing is to create an informational desert in which library users have to find their own oases – usually by presenting the library staff with the all-too-familiar litany of redundant directional questions.

In many libraries, the task of filling this informational void is left to the staff, with no attempt being made to coordinate their efforts. This *laissez-faire* approach often results in signs that cluster around public service desks, reflecting the problems that arise there without addressing the user's need for information in more remote parts of the building. Because there is no overall planning, the signs may be inconsistent in content and form, and outdated signs may not be removed. Signs made with inadequate materials and techniques tend to be illegible from more than a few feet and to deteriorate quickly. A conglomeration of such unplanned signs, besides being confusing, can project an offhand, amateurish impression that benefits neither the user nor the library.

As an alternative to this situation, a sign system offers several advantages. Because the design process is based on a careful analysis of user needs, the resulting system can address these needs on a library-wide basis. Because terminology, layout, color, and other design elements are standardized, informational consistency as well as speed and economy in producing new signs can be achieved. Because a properly prepared system incorporates durable materials, changeable features, and a maintenance manual, its effectiveness can be constant over a long period of time. By increasing user efficiency, a sign system can lead to a decrease in the proportion of simple directional questions asked at service desks, thereby freeing the staff to deal with more substantive inquiries and possibly improving staff morale. As users become more aware of the full range of services and facilities available to them, use patterns may change. A more subtle, but equally important effect is that a comprehensive sign system establishes a consistent structure of cues in the library environment, creating not only a professional appearance but also a feeling of trust and confidence in the institution.

As with other media used in library instruction, the design of a sign system begins with consideration of its objectives -- the desired user behavior or knowledge at a given step in the search process (and, in this case, at a given location within the library building). The designer's task is then to select and develop the best possible means of achieving each objective. While any sign project necessarily involves a unique set of problems and solutions, the most common objectives of comprehensive sign systems can be grouped into six general categories: orientation, direction, identification, instruction, regulation, and current awareness. These broad objectives are discussed below along with the types of interior signs and displays that might be used to achieve them.

ORIENTATION

A user entering the library or moving from one area to another needs to identify and select relevant resources and establish their general locations within the building. The sign system should respond to the user's need to progress from general to specific information during this process.

Main lobby directories listing library resources, areas, and services and relating them to a building map.

Displays in specific areas, such as elevator lobbies on stack floors, providing more detailed orientation to these areas.

Self-guided tours, in printed or cassette form, keyed to marked locations in the building.

DIRECTION

The user needs to make correct wayfinding decisions as he/she moves along the route from starting point to destination. This process demands careful attention in libraries where resources are spread out or architecturally hidden, and where the user often has a series of tasks to perform.

Directional signs placed at decision points, i.e., wherever significant numbers of users have to make wayfinding choices or change direction.

IDENTIFICATION

The user (who may not be able to distinguish one library resource, tool, or service point from another based on appearance alone) needs to recognize his/her destination upon arrival. Since some destinations are more heavily used or must be seen from farther away than others, identification signs are usually designed in a hierarchy of sign sizes or type sizes.

Large signs, supergraphics, or color coding to mark major areas.
Signs giving numbers and names of individual rooms and offices.
Signs identifying special facilities for handicapped users.
Signs identifying specific library tools; these may also display instructional information as discussed below.
Stack end labels and other signs identifying particular parts of the library collection.

INSTRUCTION

The user, having arrived at a particular resource, needs to know what to expect from it and how to use it effectively. The aim here is to present basic information as clearly as possible, reinforcing what the user may have learned about search strategy through other forms of library instruction, and, where appropriate, reminding the user that the staff is available for further assistance.

Information displays at major tools – card catalogs, public-access computer terminals, and reference sources or groups of sources such as periodical indexes. This type of display is especially important with the advent of COM and online catalogs, computerized literature searching, and other developments requiring significant changes in user behavior.
Point-of-use presentations in audio-visual or printed form, coordinated with the graphics in design, content, and placement.
Displays designed to give an overall view of search strategy or library procedures; less common than the above but certainly possible.
Signs explaining specific procedures at circulation desks and similar locations, as needed.
Exhibits calling attention to particular library resources.
Suggestion/response boards, an excellent communications tool which can incorporate graphic elements consistent with the rest of the system.

REGULATION

The user needs to know what behavior is forbidden, permitted, or required in a particular area or situation. With careful planning, a library can often reduce the number of regulatory signs while at the same time clarifying their messages. The use of symbols, color, size, or placement to distinguish regulatory signs from other signs should be considered.

Signs regarding smoking, food/beverages, noise, and security procedures.

Signs showing fire exit routes, emergency procedures, meeting room capacities, or other information required by building codes.

Copyright notices posted at copy machines.

CURRENT AWARENESS

The user needs to know about temporary conditions or changes in the library that might affect his/her tasks, as well as library hours, special events, and similar information. This objective can be a-chieved through making parts of the system changeable and the current information recognizable as such.

Bulletin boards for posting of current information, located in high traffic areas, perhaps on or near the major orientation directories.

A consistent format for library notices so that users will recognize them at once.

Provision for listing "Changes" on or adjacent to library floor plans and directories.

Posting of explanatory notices at locations in the building where changes (e.g., shifting of books) are taking place.

Incorporation of changeable text strips or panels into signs and displays where information is likely to change frequently.

One of the most essential parts of any sign system is not a sign at all, but rather a maintenance manual which describes the entire system and each of its component sign types, giving guidelines for cleaning, re-ordering, installation, and other necessary tasks. The staff members responsible for maintaining the system can follow this manual to ensure that the basic design of the system will remain consistent even when the information presented does change.

As the foregoing discussion suggests, informational graphics and sign systems can play an important role in educating the library user. They are "on the job" any time the library is open, reaching even those users who have had no other instruction. They can perform a number of functions, from orienting users to the library's resources and services to presenting specific instructional information at the point of need. They can affect the kinds of interactions users have with the staff and the ways in which users perceive the library itself.

The consequences of over-reliance on signs and graphics, however, may be just as serious as the consequences of neglect. Signs cannot convey the subtleties of reference sources or the conceptual framework necessary for successful research as effectively as a well-planned bibliographic instruction session. They cannot involve the user in an active role as effectively as exercises, workbooks, or interactive computer programs. They cannot serve as portable reference aids as effectively as printed guides and bibliographies. Their role is different from -- and complementary to -- those of the other media.

Thus, no instructional medium should be seen as a substitute for the others; especially when staff time and resources are at a premium, all applicable media should be designed to work together for maximum effect. A sign system can provide the reinforcement that links the conceptual and factual content of bibliographic instruction to the library environment in which the user must actually operate from day to day. If the graphics incorporate elements of form, content, and terminology that also occur in the library's verbal, audio-visual, and printed instructional presentations, the user will be encouraged to remember and apply what he/she has learned. The only way to achieve this synergistic effect, other than by chance, is through a unified design program that recognizes the proper function of each medium.

There is a need for further research and communication in the evolving field of library graphics. Systematic research on the effectiveness of various forms of information display in library settings would be useful. Libraries which have installed sign systems can perform a considerable service by documenting both their designs and their experiences. Conferences and workshops -- particularly those which bring librarians and designers together -- can play an important role in advancing the state of the art.

The most fundamental need, however, is for individual libraries and library staffs to undertake the task of providing their users with coherent and useful information in graphic form. Those who do will find that both they and their user will benefit from the effort.

NOTES

1. A more extensive version of these remarks is to appear in the *Drexel Library Quarterly*, vol. 16, no. 1, tentatively scheduled for Fall 1980.

2. Association of Research Libraries, Office of Management Studies, Systems and Procedures Exchange Center, "External Communication in ARL Libraries," *SPEC Flyer No. 56* (July--August 1979).

SELECTED BIBLIOGRAPHY

Carey, R.J.P., *Library Guiding: A Program for Exploiting Library Resources*. London: Clive Bingley, 1974.

Cohen, Aaron and Elaine Cohen, *Designing and Space Planning for Libraries: A Behavioral Guide*. New York: Bowker, 1979.

Crosby/Fletcher/Forbes, *A Sign Systems Manual*. London: Studio Vista, 1970.

Follis, John and Dave Hammer, *Architectural Signing and Graphics*. New York: Whitney Library of Design, 1979.

Kosterman, Wayne, "A Guide to Library Environmental Graphics." *Library Technology Reports* 14 (May--June 1978): 269--95.

Pollet, Dorothy, "You Can Get There from Here: New Directions in Library Signage," *Wilson Library Bulletin* 50 (February 1976): 456--62.

Pollet, Dorothy and Peter Haskell, eds., *Sign Systems for Libraries: Solving the Wayfinding Problem*. New York: Bowker, 1979.

Spencer, Herbert and Linda Reynolds, *Directional Signing and Labelling in Libraries and Museums: A Review of Current Theory and Practice*. London: Readability of Print Research Unit. Royal College of Art, 1977.

APPENDIX

Checklist: Objectives and components of library sign systems.

ORIENTATION	Main lobby directories. Directories for specific floors and areas. Self-guided tours.
DIRECTION	Directional signs at "decision points" on major routes.
IDENTIFICATION	Large signs marking major areas and service points. Signs identifying individual rooms. Signs marking facilities for handicapped users. Signs marking parts of the library collection.
INSTRUCTION	Point-of-use information displays at major library tools: card catalogs, public-access computer terminals, periodical indexes, etc. Displays giving an overall view of search strategy or library procedures. Signs explaining specific procedures, e.g , at circulation desks. Exhibits calling attention to library resources. Suggestion/response boards.
REGULATION	Signs regulating behavior, e.g., "No Smoking." Signs required by building or fire codes. Copyright notices at copy machines.
CURRENT AWARENESS	Bulletin boards for current information. Recognizable format for library notices. Posting of explanatory notices where major changes are occurring. Procedures for updating information on signs.

COMPUTER--ASSISTED INSTRUCTION IN LIBRARIES: PAST, PRESENT, AND FUTURE

Mary Huston-Miyamoto
Evergreen State College

The computer is one of this century's most important and pervasive technological developments. It is the most all-purpose machine in existence; the scope of computer operations is only limited by one's ability to write a program directing the machine to execute a given function. The seventies saw the computer in the library transformed from a novelty to an irreplaceable component of many operations in both public and technical services. Commonplace library applications of computerization include acquisition, cataloging, and circulation systems, and online information storage and retrieval. Less common has been the utilization of the computer in the delivery of library instruction.

The topic of the following paper will be the past, present, and future applications of this important instruction medium. In the first half of this paper I will discuss the scope of computer-aided education; descriptions of applications of computerization in library instruction will suggest the range of approaches which have been implemented to date. In the concluding section of the presentation, I will show that changing demands on libraries suggest that an important role will be assumed by computer-assisted instruction in the eighties.

Background

Computers can be utilized in instruction in a variety of ways. In the context of computer-assisted instruction (CAI), the computer acts "as middleman between instructor and student. The computer accepts and stores information from the instructor, produces it upon demand from the student, and guides the student through prescribed learning sequences"[1] at his or her own pace.

The simplest application of CAI is linear programmed instruction. The student is given a unit of instruction and then tested. The computer judges the answer and generates an appropriate response. Regardless of individual performance, each student is presented

99

identical instruction content. Using the computer in this way -- primarily as a "page turner" -- does not adequately exploit its capabilities.

More sophisticated instructional design accommodates the individualization of each student's educational experience. By incorporating branching, each student can be routed to appropriate parts of the lesson based on his or her learning needs. Individualization is an integral component of good CAI lessons.

> Still more imaginative programs have been developed, which rely on the simulation capabilities of a computer. Medical students have been taught diagnosis using a computer: given a hypothetical patient with certain symptoms, the student makes a diagnosis and prescribes a course of treatment. If a fatal mistake is made, the patient is, after all, only hypothetical . . . . On the PLATO system, developed at the University of Illinois . . . education majors can simulate a first year of teaching: given a principal with unknown characteristics, the students make a series of decisions and find out at the end of a hypothetical year whether they are fired, retained, or promoted. Such creative applications of CAI carry their own intrinsic motivation. Students learn almost despite themselves.[2]

Responding in part to improvements in hardware capabilities,* libraries have developed some valuable instructional software.[3] Among the major projects during the last decade are those at the University of Denver, the University of Arizona,[4] the Ohio State University,[5] and the University of Illinois at Urbana-Champaign.[6]

Past and Present CAI Applications

The CAI project at the University of Denver[7] is the best documented in library literature. The experiment was first considered when the staff realized that traditional instructional methods were inadequate. In an attempt to solve these problems, the University of Denver Libraries adopted CAI on an experimental basis in 1971 as part of a comprehensive library orientation and instruction program. The scope of the twenty-one lesson courseware package was broad, ranging from instruction on accessing book reviews and biographies to utilizing periodical indexes and abstracts. A tutorial mode of

---

* Another factor influencing the development of CAI courseware was the availability of generous federal funding in the 1960's and early 1970's. As sources of external funding diminished, so did much of the experimentation with this instructional medium.

instruction was employed: the computer presented explanatory material which was followed by questions testing the student's understanding of the information. For a question answered incorrectly, the student was provided with additional explanation and then questioned again. Handouts on the topics were placed next to the terminal, thereby reducing the need for notetaking during the instructional episode and providing material supplementary to the basic skills mastered through CAI. Patron evaluations demonstrated that a significant segment of the user population was reached and reacted favorably to this instructional approach. The courseware was available 18 hours each day and proved to be a good complement to traditional instructional approaches[8] concurrently available in the Libraries.

A second CAI project will be described in more depth, beginning with a brief review of its origin. The Library Computer System (LCS) became operational at the University of Illinois at Urbana-Champaign in December 1978.[9] The database consists of records from the Library's shelflist. Both circulation transactions and known-item searches can be conducted in an online mode by staff members at LCS terminals.[10]

Library users can also search the database at public terminals. Because LCS was not primarily designed for public use, there are no built-in search aids -- such as system prompts -- to guide the user through the search. When LCS first became operational at Illinois, two methods of instruction were available for patrons wishing to learn the searching procedures. They could refer to the printed instructions posted next to each public terminal. This approach, however, assumed a familiarity with computer operations which not all patrons possessed. A second option was to ask a library staff member for instruction. Obviously, one-to-one instruction for each potential new user on a campus of over 35,000 students is a very labor intensive proposition. It was apparent to the University Librarian Hugh Atkinson that an additional form of instruction had to be developed.

I was asked to design and program appropriate CAI material for new searchers on LCS. A basic courseware package is now operational on the PLATO computer-based education system. (PLATO is the acronym for Programmed Logic for Automated Teaching Operations.) However, additional refinements in branching options must still be made. My feeling that the lesson is still not finished is due, in part, to the sophistication of the system: PLATO could be described as the Cadillac of instructional computing.[11] "Imagine an educational tool that combines the verbal interactions of the telephone, the graphic capability of animation, the visual display of a television screen, the supportive assistance of a teacher, and the self-paced format of programmed instruction, and what you get is PLATO!"[12]

Preparatory to developing the courseware package, the needs of the academic community were first studied. As the instructional designer for the project, I talked extensively with subject experts in the Library concerning the basics which must be mastered for minimum competency in LCS searching. Simultaneously, a study was conducted which identified errors commonly contributing to unsuccessful searches by library users.[13] In defining the behavioral objectives for the PLATO lesson, I relied heavily on the information provided from both these sources.

In designing the software, I utilized PLATO's system capabilities to maximize instructional effectiveness. The following are lesson features which a student might experience in a typical instructional episode. Upon signing on to the PLATO system, a student is presented with a menu of lesson options. When the lesson on LCS searching strategy is selected, the student is routed to the title page of the LCS lesson and instructed to press the NEXT key on the keyboard to advance. (See Screen Display 1.)* The following frame allows students without previous experience on PLATO to enter the portion of the lesson with instructions on the functions of keyboard keys. Since over half the student body at the University of Illinois have used PLATO, many students will elect to go directly to the next screen display which outlines the goals and objectives of this lesson. Students are advised that following completion of the lesson they should know how to borrow library material using LCS as well as how to conduct general and detailed searches on public LCS terminals. All students are then routed to the lesson index which outlines the arrangement of the lesson. (See Screen Display 2.) A student may select any section of the lesson but – for the sake of illustration – let's assume that he or she decides to begin with number 2, the section on general searches. The learner would then type a "2," press the NEXT key, and see a frame which explains command syntax.

Several screen displays later, the student is presented with a listing of command codes for general searches. (See Screen Display 3.) This frame illustrates simple but appropriate application of PLATO's graphic capabilities. The underlining is of mnemonic value in reminding the student that, for example, the title search code (TLS) is a composite of the "t" and "l" from "title" and the "s" from "search." A more sophisticated application of the TUTOR language's "draw" command is used at another point in the lesson

---

* Screen display reproductions follow the Notes at the end of the paper.

to identify the elements of the LCS record through numbers in boxes which correspond to numbered labels at the bottom of the screen. The LCS record is written in sized writing, both to set it apart from the text and to replicate more closely the script actually used in an LCS transaction. (See Screen Display 4.)

In the LCS lesson, a question is presented after every 1 to 3 screen displays of text. The question which follows the page identifying record elements requires the student to categorize an item enclosed in a box. At the end of the lesson is an optional review which requires a higher level of problem solving on the part of the learner. One of the questions presented to the student in the review test requires that the learner understands several aspects of searching on LCS and is intended to assess cumulative understanding: given partial bibliographic information for the bestseller *The World According to Garp*, a student must identify possible searching strategies on LCS. If the student answered incorrectly, PLATO provides both the correct answer and an explanation of the student's error. (See Screen Display 5.)

A multiple choice response mechanism was selected for the questions to allow for expansion of the lesson into a multiple branched style format that routes individuals based on their response choice (which indicates remediation or advancement). This format also facilitates item analysis of each question: accumulated data can be used to assess the effectiveness of each response alternative.

At any point in the lesson, the learner may return to the index to select another section of instruction; he or she may also back up in the lesson to review the preceding lesson material. Any student signed on to the lesson may also send comments to me from any page of the lesson; comments are collected in "lcsnotes," a PLATO notes file. To date, I have received over 50 suggestions, many of which I incorporated into lesson revisions.

Demographic data is also collected from the user population by means of a short questionnaire. One question asks the students about their experience using LCS; this information will be useful in determining if the level of the courseware corresponds to the searching sophistication of the students. The demographic data and student performance data are displayed on charts which I can call up from any page in the lesson. The performance data, the users' profile, and online student comments will be used in further evaluating and revising the lesson content.

What advantages do the CAI programs at Denver and Illinois share with other computer-assisted instruction efforts? One advantage of this medium involves the computer's responsiveness to the individual learner. Computer-based teaching systems can accommodate complex instructional strategies with multiple branching capabilities which are adaptable to the student's level of knowledge. In addition, the learner can execute the lesson at the time it is needed when motivation is highest. He or she has control over the speed with which information is presented, and is also provided with immediate feedback on responses to review and test questions.

An additional advantage of CAI is the computer's ability to store a record of students' behavior for use in performance diagnosis and lesson evaluation. Also, programs may be easily updated or modified once they are stored in the computer.* CAI can potentially remove repetitive instruction from librarians, thereby freeing us to respond to more unique informational needs. While educational technology will not replace personal contact with librarians, it can augment and enrich our teaching efforts.

The CAI projects operational during the past decade at Denver, Illinois, Arizona, and Ohio have shown that CAI is a viable means of providing orientation and instruction to library users. Through a variety of instructional designs for a number of different topics, the instructional potential of the computer has been utilized to deliver self-paced, individualized education. To both conclude this section and to introduce a subject which I will be discussing in the conclusion of this paper, I should like to describe two other CAI efforts -- Individualized Instruction for Data Access (IIDA) and MED-- LEARN. Both courseware packages are designed to make online bibliographic systems more accessible to end-users.[14]

IIDA has been jointly developed by Drexel University and the Franklin Institute. Its primary audience is direct users of scientific and technical information systems, typically scientists and engineers who perform a few bibliographic searches per year. In addition to providing conventional CAI material, the IIDA program monitors student-computer interaction, evaluates the users' performance, communicates information about detected errors, and suggests ways to proceed. This system offers users both an alternative to using an intermediary for basic searches and preparation for working more effectively with an intermediary for the most difficult searches.[15]

Another noteworthy effort in this area is the National Library of Medicine's MEDLEARN program. This software package provides tutorial dialogue, drill and practice, and testing. In addition, two MEDLINE simulations are included, providing the student with an opportunity to formulate and execute a search and to have it evaluated before performing the search in MEDLINE.[16]

----

*   Many of the same benefits can be cited for computer-assisted test construction (CATC). See Appendix A for a description of a successful testing program implemented at Virginia Polytechnic Institute and State University, Blacksburg, Virginia.

These two CAI projects are important prototypes for future design of instructional components for online systems. Although library literature contains some reports on instructional programs to teach end-users, insufficient attention has generally been given to this requirement for efficient online searching. Successful introduction of patrons to an ever-increasing online mode of accessing information requires that we begin *now* to consider the best approaches to instruction.* In the next section of this paper, I will discuss the role that I envision for CAI in the context of our future library and information environment.

Future CAI Applications

Advances in technology have produced computers with increasingly sophisticated capabilities; computing costs are decreasing even while capabilities are increasing. Online computer systems have already demonstrated new dimensions of access for abstracting and indexing database services; technological advances have resulted in the widespread introduction of online bibliographic systems in libraries and information centers. Futurists predict that information seekers will increasingly be consulting the machine-readable records of bibliographic, full text, numeric, and referral databases to satisfy their information needs. (The costs of maintaining paper records are increasing and the limitations of this format are becoming increasingly apparent.)

I see the marriage of online information systems and interactive

---

*   In anticipation of widespread direct interrogation of online catalogs by faculty and students, The Research Libraries Group at Stanford University is developing a prototype patron access system. Both computer-assisted training modules and the reference staff of the participating research libraries will be available for teaching faculty and students to utilize the computer interface to the catalog. (Interview with Doug Ferguson, The Research Libraries Group, Inc., Stanford University, Palo Alto, California, April 1980.)

Another approach to facilitating user access to online catalog information is operational in Canada at the University of Waterloo Library in Ontario. The prototype system, the Community Access Module (CAM), has a CAI component which is integrated into the software package for the catalog. The instructional content is modified on an ongoing basis in response to both formal and informal evaluations of users' searching performance. (Interview with Gerry Meek, Orientation Librarian, Library, University of Waterloo, Waterloo, Ontario, Canada, May 1980.)

computer-assisted instruction modules as being of major importance in future applications of CAI. CAI has already been shown to be an effective technique for teaching searchers of online bibliographic systems.* Involvement with CAI by the beginning searcher has the further advantage of offering the novice familiarity with the online medium and exercise in developing appropriate psychomotor skills. Hence, learning transfer can occur. This logic was recognized as long ago as 1975 when Dineh Moghdam noted that CAI is the most promising form of instruction for online retrieval systems, in that medium as well as message may be used to acquaint the beginning searcher with an interactive user/system interface.[17] Although a significant investment of time and money is required to develop good CAI material, the expense could be cost-effective in terms of the number of potential users of the courseware and the inherent compatibility of these two products of online technology.[18] Co-operative efforts[19] between network representatives or database vendors, librarian consultants, and CAI authors could insure that courseware is developed which meets the instructional needs of the end-user population.

In conclusion, then, the seventies have been a time of experimentation with computer-assisted instruction in libraries. Considering the growing number of information consumers who will be querying online information systems directly,[20] it is essential that we begin immediately to develop appropriate instructional material,[21] learning from our past experiences to fully utilize the potential of educational technology in maximizing the information systems of the future.

----

* CAI could also be successfully applied to staff training for computerized operations. Little attention has yet been given to this area, however. See Appendix B for a memorandum recommending adoption of CAI for staff training on LCS at the University of Illinois: the document outlines the instructional components of the proposed software package.

NOTES

1. Culkin, Patricia B. "Computer-Assisted Instruction in Library Use," *Drexel Library Quarterly* 8 (July 1972): 301.

2. Adams, Mignon. "Individualized Approach to Library Skills Development," *Library Trends* 29 (Summer 1980): 83–94.

3. Although not within the scope of this paper, several important

CAI projects have also been operational in library schools during the last decade. The following are references to the major experiments: Chan, Lois M. "Computer-Assisted Instruction in DDC," *Journal of Education for Librarianship* 16 (Summer 1975): 33–40. Meredith, J.C. "Machine-Assisted Approach to General Reference Materials," *Journal of the American Society for Information Science* 22 (May--June 1971): 176--186. Penland, Patrick R. "Continuing Education in a Problem Solving Model," *Special Libraries* 66 (February 1975): 55--60. Slavens, Thomas P. "The Development and Testing of Materials for Computer-Assisted Instruction in the Education of Reference Librarians," *RQ* 13 (Fall 1973): 15--18. Starks, David D., Horn, Barbara J., Slavens, Thomas P. "Two Modes of Computer Assisted Instruction in a Library Reference Course," *Journal of the American Society for Information Science* 23 (July--August 1972): 271--277.

4. Robson, John, Carolyn Kacena and Charles Peters. "PLATO IV Comes of Age," *Network* 1 (July 1974): 12–14.

5. Clark, Alice S. "Computer Assisted Instruction in Use of the Library: One Solution for the Large University." In *A Challenge for Academic Libraries: How to Motivate Students to Use the Library*, ed. by Sul H. Lee. Ann Arbor, MI: Pierian Press, 1973, pp. 58–62.

6. Three of the science departmental libraries at the University of Illinois at Urbana-Champaign have developed CAI orientation/instruction modules. The courseware is described in the following references: Davis, Elizabeth B., et al. "A Two-Phased Model for Library Instruction," *Bulletin of the Medical Library Association* 65 (January 1977): 40--45. Hicks, Joan Tomay. "Computer-Assisted Instruction in Library Orientation and Services," *Bulletin of the Medical Library Association* 64 (April 1976): 238--240. Williams, Mitsuko and Elisabeth B. Davis, "Evaluation of PLATO Library Instructional Lessons," *The Journal of Academic Librarianship* 5 (March 1979): 14--19. Another notable study discussed the comparative effectiveness of CAI and the lecture method in teaching library use techniques: Axeen, Maureen. *Teaching Library Use to Undergraduates: Comparison of Computer-Based Instruction and the Conventional Lecture (Final Report)*. Bethesda, MD: ERIC Document Reproduction Service, ED 014 316, 1967.

7. Culkin, Patricia. "Computer-Assisted Instruction in Library Use," *Drexel Library Quarterly* 8 (July 1972): 301–311. See also:

Culkin, Patricia B. "CAI Experiment," *American Libraries* 3 (June 1972): 643–645.

8. For discussion of mediums used in library instruction programs, consult the following references: Dudley, Miriam. "Teaching Library Skills to College Students." In *Advances in Librarianship*, ed. by M.J. Voigt. New York: Seminar Press, 1972, pp. 86–92. Fjällbrant, Nancy. "Teaching Methods for the Education of the Library User," *Libri* 26 (December 1976): 254–266. Stoffle, Carla J. and Gabriella Bonn. "An Inventory of Library Orientation and Instruction Methods," *RQ* 13 (Winter 1973): 129–133.

9. The first implementation of LCS occurred at the Ohio State University. For a discussion of the initial system consult: Atkinson, Hugh C. "The Ohio State On-Line Circulation System." In *Proceedings of the 1972 Clinic on Library Applications of Data Processing*, ed. by F. Wilfrid Lancaster. Urbana, Illinois, April 30–May 3, 1972, pp. 22–28. Urbana: University of Illinois Graduate School of Library Science, 1972.

10. Additional information on the Library Computer System at the University of Illinois can be obtained from: Corey, James F. and Lynne M. Blair. "The Library Computer System at the University of Illinois," *Illinois Libraries* 60 (April 1978): 365–371. See also: Atkinson, Hugh C. "LCS, Its Future," *Illinois Libraries* 60 (April 1978): 371–374.

11. The features of this computer-based education system are described more fully in the following brochure: Computer-Based Education Research Laboratory. "The PLATO System." Urbana: University of Illinois at Urbana-Champaign, 1979. Some exciting research and development work on PLATO promises even more sophisticated system capabilities in the future. Of special significance in teaching the visually handicapped are the speech synthesis capabilities being developed by Maggs and Sherwood. These references discuss their work to date: Maggs, Peter. "Access to CAI for the Blind and Visually Handicapped." In *Proceedings of the Annual Convention of the Association for the Development of Computer-Based Instructional Systems*, San Diego, February 27–March 1, 1979, vol. 3, pp. 436–445. Sherwood, Bruce A. "The Computer Speaks," *IEEE Spectrum* 16 (August 1979): 18–25. Sherwood, Bruce A. "Fast Text-to-Speech Algorithms for Esperanto, Spanish, Italian, Russian, and English," *International Journal of Man-Machine Studies* 10

(1978): 669–692.

12. Correspondence from Beth Dankert, Eugene W. Stetson Memorial Library, Mercer University, Macon, Georgia, April 1980.

13. Specht, Jerry. "Patron Use of an Online Circulation System in Known-Item Searching." *Journal of the American Society for Information Science* 31 (September 1980): 335–346.

14. An online training package is also being developed at the University of Pittsburgh for potential users of Lockheed/DIALOG and SDC/ORBIT. See: Caruso, Elaine and John Griffiths. "A TRAINER for Online Systems," *Online* 1 (October 1977): 28–34.

15. Meadow, C.T. and Epstein B.E. "Individualized Instruction for Data Access." In *Proceedings of the First International On-Line Information Meeting.* London, December 13–15, 1977, pp. 179–194. Oxford: Learned Information Ltd., 1977. See also: Meadow, Charles T. "The Computer as a Search Intermediary," *Online* 3 (July 1979): 54–59.

16. Eisenberg, Laura J., et al. "MEDLEARN: A Computer-Assisted Instruction (CAI) Program for MEDLARS," *Bulletin of the Medical Library Association* 66 (January 1978): 6–13.

17. Moghdam, Dineh. "User Training for On-Line Information Retrieval Systems," *Journal of the American Society for Information Science* 26 (May–June 1975): 184–188.

18. Assessing cost-effectiveness is further discussed in: Avner, R.A. "Cost-Effective Applications of Computer-Based Education," *Educational Technology* 18 (April 1978): 24–26.

19. The increasing electronic information environment will impact significantly on libraries during the coming decade. Changing student populations and increasing fiscal constraints in academic institutions during the 1980's will also force changes in library services. Even as we're experiencing declining budgets, we'll be asked to provide outreach services to an increasingly diverse clientele, many of whom may be part-time, older learners who are receiving instruction in "classrooms" remote from the campus. Libraries must exhibit flexibility in providing informational services at times and places convenient to the changing student population. There is potential for exploring cooperative development of CAI courseware on basic library skills. Jointly developed

instructional material could be shared through networking or through software clearinghouses. For a discussion of appropriate CAI courseware development, see: Yamada, Ken. "Contemporary Library Strategy and Computer Assisted Individualized Learning," *Tennessee Librarian* 26 (Summer/Fall 1974): 84--87. The feasibility of a software clearinghouse is discussed in: Dunnagan, Trinka. "Considering a Clearinghouse for Computer-Based Curriculum Materials." In *Proceedings of the 37th ASIS Annual Meeting*, ed. by Pranas Zunde. Atlanta, Georgia, October 13--17, 1974, pp. 218--222.

20. Meadow, Charles T. "Online Searching and Computer Programming -- Some Behavioral Similarities (Or . . . Why End Users Will Eventually Take Over the Terminal)," *Online* 3 (January 1979): 49--52.

21. A successful multimedia program is operational at Chalmers University of Technology Library in Gothenburg, Sweden. For a discussion of its scope and instructional features, see: Fjällbrant, Nancy and Sture Hard. "Design and Evaluation of Multimedia Programmes for Education in On-Line Information Retrieval," *Tidskrift For Dukumentction--The Scandinavian Documentation Journal* 35 (1979): 101--106.

To prepare for our electronic future, we must also give consideration to the requirements for "computer searching literacy" -- to understanding concepts characteristic of online information systems and search processes. One method of accomplishing this is proposed in: Huston-Miyamoto, Mary and Susan Smith. "Putting the Cart before the Horse Instruction of Online Users." Olympia, WA: The Evergreen State College, April 1980. (Mimeographed.)

SCREEN DISPLAY 1

The source of these computer screen displays is a program written for the CERL Plato System; displays are reproduced by permission and through the courtesy of the University of Illinois.

INDEX

In this lesson, you may advance through the
sections in the order designated below. You may
also select only those topics in which you are
interested. (Throughout the lesson, you may return
to the Index by pressing down the ▨ key while
holding down the ▬ key.) Type the number of the
section where you wish to begin. Then press ▨.

1. INTRODUCTION TO LCS

2. GENERAL SEARCHES

   3. TITLE SEARCHES

   4. AUTHOR/TITLE SEARCHES

   5. AUTHOR SEARCHES

   6. SHELFLIST POSITION SEARCHES

7. DETAILED SEARCHES

8. SERIAL SEARCHES

9. CIRCULATION

   ❯

SCREEN DISPLAY 2

Each of the searches has a command code which tells the computer which procedure to perform.

TLS/	=	TITLE SEARCH
ATS/	=	AUTHOR-TITLE SEARCH
AUS/	=	AUTHOR SEARCH
SPS/	=	SHELF POSITION SEARCH
DSC/	=	DETAILED SEARCH BY CALL NUMBER
DSL/	=	DETAILED SEARCH BY LINE NUMBER

To perform a search on LCS,

1)   enter the command code (message identifier);

2)   separate the parts of the search request message with a slash;

3)   enter the search code (portions of the title and/or author of the desired item);

4)   press the RETURN key.

SCREEN DISPLAY 3

In conducting a search for which there is only one "match," you will receive information on the item's circulation status and library location(s), in addition to its bibliographical information. The elements of the record which you will find most useful are identified below.

| 1 | | 2 | | 3 | 4 |

301.4242H12@   HAHN, EMILY ONCE UPON A PEDESTAL@NY   74-5354

131615   1974 | 5 | 4 | 6 | ADDED: 7@@221

@1   @@1   2W   IUX
@2   @@2   3W   UGX
@3   @@3   16-4W   EDX   CHGD   79@314/79@7@4   UC
@4   @@4   16-4W   STX

| 7 | 8 | | 9 | 1@ | 11 | 12 | 13 | 14 |

1   call number   8   volume number
2   author   9   copy number
3   title   1@   loan period
4   place of publication   11   holding libraries*
5   date of publication   12   circulation status
6   total no. of copies   13   date charged out
7   line number   14   date due

* A listing of the libraries and their abbrev-
iations on LCS is posted next to every terminal.

SCREEN DISPLAY 4

Try this question over the previous material.

If you wished to borrow the novel The World According to Garp and knew that the book was written by John Irving, all but one of the following search strategies would correctly search the LCS database. Which answer is incorrect?

1. AUS/IRVING,ᴊJOHN
2. ATS/IRVITHE
3. TLS/WORLACCOR
4. AUS/IRVING,ᴊJ

> 1

Only number 2 is incorrect; "the" is considered to be a "non-significant" word when conducting a LCS search. "IRVIWORLD" would be the correct search code for an ATS.
Press NEXT to continue

SCREEN DISPLAY 5

APPENDIX A

Excerpts from "An Approach to Freshman Library Instruction: Computer Produced/Scored Exercises." University Libraries General Reference Division, Virginia Polytechnic Institute and State University, Blacksburg, Virginia.

During the fall quarter, four thousand freshmen are introduced to Newman Library services and resources. The initial orientation is accomplished by means of a slide-tape presentation and a classroom discussion conducted by a librarian.

However, the main feature of the Freshman Library Program is a library exercise. Four thousand unique exercises are produced through a computer program. Each item in the exercise is related to a specific objective previously discussed in the classroom. In order to complete the twenty item exercise, students must see the *Library of Congress Subject Headings List*, card catalogs, newspaper and periodical indexes and microforms. Thirty variations of each item provide a large file from which the computer randomly selects, combines and generates the exercises.

Each student receives an exercise and an optical-scan answer sheet . . . . Upon completing the exercise, the students turn in the op-scan sheet and receive the answer key for this exercise as well as a generalized answer guide. This immediate feedback enables students to receive immediate reinforcement from their learning experience. Each instructor receives a print-out reporting their students' scores and mistakes . . . .

A computer programmed exercise and a computer scored answer sheet has advantages for students, librarians and . . . faculty. The question file can be easily added to, modified and refined. It is possible to divide the exercise into instructional modules for use in more specific areas of bibliographic instruction. The computer scored answer sheet provides efficient and accurate correction of the exercises which is extremely important when large numbers of students are involved. The data from the answer sheets is easily collected and analyzed. Data from the program will be used in an item analysis in order to improve future applications of this approach to library instruction.

(Received in April 1980 from William W. Prince [formerly Head, General Reference Division, Newman Library, Virginia Polytechnic Institute and State University], presently Head, Undergraduate Library, SUNY/Buffalo, who also credits Donald Kenney and Joann Eustis as co-authors of the exercise program.)

APPENDIX B

STAFF TRAINING ON LCS

(Memorandum circulated internally at the Library of the University of Illinois at Urbana-Champaign by Mary Huston-Miyamoto in May 1979.)

PLATO is recommended as the medium of instruction for training library staff (student workers, support staff, and librarians) to utilize the Library Computer System (LCS) for searches and circulation of items in the shelflist data base. The choice is a logical one: most people at the University of Illinois at Urbana-Champaign are familiar with PLATO and there are over 600 PLATO terminals available on campus. In addition, the computer-based education system has interactive capabilities, providing immediate answer judging and feedback and individualized branching capabilities. The appearance of an LCS transaction can be replicated on PLATO through an upper case character set or through sized writing; sophisticated graphic capabilities are also available. The courseware could also be used on a cooperative basis with other institutions adopting LCS and having PLATO terminals connected to the Computer-Based Education Research Lab (CERL) network.

General behavioral objectives have been developed for both search and circulation procedures. Commonly made search errors were identified through a one-month study of over 600 search transactions.[1] Difficulties in performing circulation transactions on LCS were identified by an LCS Training Committee member experienced in training staff to operate the system. A set of specific objectives for each group of library employees must next be developed; students, for instance, would not need to know as many procedures as librarians.

The development of an educationally effective CAI program requires expertise in the subject content, in instructional design, and in computer programming. Following consultation with experts in these areas, the following software package for teaching the library staff is proposed.

Two tutorial style lessons will be developed to present detailed instruction on circulation and search procedures. Staff members will

---

1. Specht, Jerry. "Patron Use of an Online Circulation System in Known-Item Searching." Accepted for publication in the *Journal of the American Society for Information Science.* (In press.)

indicate their status upon signing on to the system; this will be the basis for routing them to sections cf the lessons appropriate for their position. Instruction will be in an interactive mode with alternating presentation of information and questions. A multiple choice response mechanism is recommended for the questions to allow for expansion of the lesson into a branched style format which routes individuals based on their response choice (which indicates remediation or advancement). This format also facilitates item analysis of each question: accumulated data could be used to assess the effectiveness of response alternatives. The performance data could also be used to identify sections within the lesson which need revision. Additional user feedback can be obtained through a PLATO system feature which allows users to send comments online to the lesson author. These comments can be analyzed to further refine the effectiveness of the instructional presentation.

A drill and practice will follow each tutorial lesson; the drills will reinforce instruction on message identifiers and command syntax and facilitate quick recall of these procedures. Code will be developed which will individualize each drill based on the person's performance -- i.e., the individual will be presented with items similar to those most often missed in the preceding portion of the drill as well as with items reviewing new material.

Following adequate collection of data to identify common misunderstandings/problems made in using LCS, a simulation style lesson will be developed to allow staff to further investigate the procedures necessary for the operation of LCS. The simulation of LCS procedures will allow staff to explore consequences in a nonpunitive environment; they will thereby better understand the correct procedures. By exploring the procedural environment, staff members will learn to develop optimum solution procedures and to avoid (or remedy) errors when actually in the real life situation.

Each staff member's progress through this series of lessons will be directed by a computer managed instruction (CMI) program which will record each user's performance in the instructional modules and will automatically route the person to the next lesson following mastery. The CMI software package will handle all the record keeping for the training of library staff on LCS.

Employing a CMI framework and CAI courseware would largely relieve librarians from training responsibilities for LCS and allow them to concentrate on other professional activities.

LIBRARY ORIENTATION AND INSTRUCTION -- 1979

Hannelore B. Rader
Coordinator
Education and Psychology Division
Center of Educational Resources
Eastern Michigan University

The following annotated bibliography of materials on orienting users to the library and on instructing them in the use of reference and other resources covers publications from 1979. A few items from 1978 were included because information about them had not been available in time for the 1978 listing. Some entries were not annotated because the compiler was unable to secure a copy of the item.

The bibliography includes publications on user instruction in all types of libraries and for all types of users from young children to adults. To facilitate the use of the list, it has been divided into categories by type of library.

Even though the library literature includes many citations to items on user instruction in foreign countries, this bibliography includes only publications in the English language.

Interest in library use instruction continues to grow as shown by the increase in publications on the topic. Compared to last year there are twenty-five percent more items in this listing.

At this time it may be of interest to the reader to observe the growth rate of publications on library use instruction since 1973 when the first of these bibliographies appeared in *Reference Services Review* 2 (January-March, 1974), pp. 91--93.

1973: 29 items; 1974: 38 items; 1975: 49 items; 1976: 69 items; 1977: 102 items; 1978: 133 items; 1979: 166 items.

Again it can be noted that some of the items appear in nonlibrary publications. Growing concern with evaluation of user instruction is evident in the increasing number of items on this topic. Even though there are still many publications on program descriptions, a growing number of the listed citations are concerned with research.

ACADEMIC LIBRARIES

COMMUNITY COLLEGE LIBRARIES

Cammack, Floyd M. "Leeward Library Offers Learning Licenses." *Community and Junior College Journal* 49 (April, 1979), pp. 32--33+.

The article describes the basic library use instruction program developed for students at Leeward Community College in Hawaii. The program materials were developed by librarians, who also administer the self-paced individualized units and the tests. The librarians also provide regular grade reports to the faculty. All of the English 100 classes are reached with this program.

Cowdrick, Charles and Robert Vuturo. *Integrated User Instruction and the Community College Library.* ERIC Document Reproduction Service, 1979. ED 168 669

The authors discuss the need and rationale for library instruction at the community college level. Various methods for providing such instruction are elaborated upon. Integrating library instruction into the curriculum is thought to be the most effective method.

Yee, Sandra G.B. "Administration of Library Instruction Programs in Michigan Community Colleges." Ph.D. dissertation, University of Michigan, 1979.

This study tried to determine the status of library instruction programs in Michigan community colleges. Three areas were studied in detail, methods of library instruction being used, how much support do these programs have from the administration and how these programs are evaluated.

COLLEGE AND UNIVERSITY LIBRARIES

Abell, Millicent D. "The Changing Role of the Academic Librarian: Drift and Mastery." *College and Research Libraries* 40 (March, 1979), pp. 154--164.

The author discusses traditional functions of the library as well as new challenges and opportunities confronting academic librarians now and in the future. The librarians' skill in mastering their professional roles is stressed. Individual initiative, willingness to engage in critical analysis and evaluation of the performance of the library and the profession will be crucial factors librarians have to deal with in the immediate future.

Allen, Ronald. *Report on Visual Display at Purdy Library. Technical Paper No. 9*. ERIC Document Reproduction Service, 1979. ED 167 130.

Presents findings of a study to evaluate effectiveness of a visual display in the form of posters on the card catalog. It was found that this was not an effective teaching method. Information should be emphasized when teaching use of sources and a different method should be used.

Baldwin, Julia F. and Robert S. Rudolph. "The Comparative Effectiveness of a Slide/Tape Show and a Library Tour." *College and Research Libraries* 40 (January, 1979), pp. 31--35.

The article describes a comparison study of a slide-tape program and the traditional library tour. One hundred fifty-one students in a freshman-level business report-writing course were tested. It was found that neither method of orientation is superior, contrary to F.F. Kuo's conclusion that the slide-tape program is better.

Berthold, Carol A. and Barbara J. Ford. *Reaching the Undergraduate with Government Publications: A Case Study in Bibliographic Instruction*. ERIC Document Reproduction Service, 1979. ED 168 465.

Describes how a documents librarian and a communications instructor cooperated at the University of Illinois to promote the use of documents through library instruction to students.

Bibliographic Instruction Handbook. Chicago: ALA ACRL Bibliographic Instruction Section, Policy and Planning Committee, 1979.

This manual developed through the cooperative efforts of the ACRL BIL Policy and Planning Committee and the ACRL Task Force on Bibliographic Instruction provides basic information and techniques for bibliographic instruction. It includes guidelines for bibliographic instruction, a needs assessment check-list, administrative considerations, timetable for programs, objectives, instructional methods, glossary of terms, a pathfinder on bibliographic instruction and an evaluation sheet.

Bibliographic Instruction Program. ERIC Document Reproduction Service, 1979. ED 169 890.

Presents objectives of the library instruction program at the University of Wisconsin--Parkside for students, faculty, community residents and staff. The program is evaluated through discussions, a skills test, evaluation forms.

Biggins, Jeanne. *A Study of the Administration of Library Use Instruction Courses by Committee.* ERIC Document Reproduction Service, 1979. ED 171 241.

This study examines the effectiveness of administering a library instruction program by a committee. The position of the committee in the library's organization, committee activity, role of the committee and committee resources were studied. Committee reports, relevant administrative documents and interviews with committee members were utilized to do this study.

Biggs, Mary M. *Course-Related and Personalized Library Instruction.* ERIC Document Reproduction Service, 1979. ED 172 724.

Describes the library instruction program at the University of Evansville where course-related instruction is planned cooperatively between librarians and teaching faculty.

Biggs, Mary M. "On My Mind -- 'The Perils of Library Instruction'--." *Journal of Academic Librarianship* 5 (July, 1979), p. 159+.

The writer points out that library instruction programs will increase the need for more space, materials and public service personnel. It has also been found that they will create personnel problems relating to scheduling, incompetence, technical services and evaluation.

Biggs, Mary M. and others. *Headpower.* 3d ed. ERIC Document Reproduction Service, 1979. ED 167 160.

This is a library handbook for freshman composition students at the University of Evansville. They are required to read this book. It covers library services and basic reference sources.

Blackburn, Robert. "Two Years with a Closed Catalog." *Journal of Academic Librarianship* 4 (January, 1979), pp. 424--429.

This paper presents the University of Toronto Library experience with a computerized card catalog system. Part of the paper describes user orientation to this type of catalog system.

Boissé, Joe. "Selling Library Instruction." *The Southeastern Librarian* 29 (Summer, 1979), pp. 81--85.

The author discusses the need to sell a library instruction program to the university administration, the faculty, the library administration, fellow librarians and students. He proposes methods of doing such a selling job.

Campbell, David E. and Theodore M. Shlechter. "Library Design Influences on User Behavior and Satisfaction." *Library Quarterly*

49 (January, 1979), pp. 26--41.

This study examined the total campus library system in relationship to user behavior. The library at the University of Kansas was used to evaluate the influences of library design on student behavior and satisfaction. Three methods were used to ascertain these influences. The conclusion states that physical design may influence student behavior and satisfaction and that the planning of libraries should be a joined effort between architects, librarians and behavioral scientists.

Davis, Jinnie Y. and Stella Bentley. "Factors Affecting Faculty Perceptions of Academic Libraries." *College and Research Libraries* 40 (November, 1979), pp. 527--532.

This article summarizes a survey of teaching faculty at three academic institutions in Worcester, MA to assess the influence of institutional affiliation, subject area, academic rank or length of time at an institution on faculty members' attitudes toward the library. Findings indicate that length of time proved the most statistically significant factor of the four. It is suggested that librarians should concentrate on working with the newer faculty members.

Flower, Clara K. *Finding Your Way: Orientation to the Library. Library Instruction Series.* Unit I. ERIC Document Reproduction Service, 1979. ED 162 664.

This is the first of three pamphlets on library skills for college students developed at the University of Maine. Its purpose is to familiarize students with the library and its services. Also provided are objectives for the library skills modules and tests.

Flower, Clara. *Finding a Book: The Card Catalog. Library Instruction Series. Unit II.* ERIC Document Reproduction Service, 1979. ED 162 665.

This is the second of three modules on library skills for college students and teaches the use of the card catalog. Tests are also provided.

Flower, Clara K. *Finding an Article: Indexes and Abstracts. Library Instruction Series. Unit III.* ERIC Document Reproduction Service, 1979. ED 162 666.

The last of three library skills modules to teach college students the use of periodical indexes and abstracts. Six tests are included.

Flower, Clara K. *Workbook. Library Instruction Series.* ERIC Document Reproduction Service, 1979. ED 162 667.

The workbook incorporates exercises to be used with Units II and III of the library skills modules for college students at the University of Maine.

Fox, Peter K. *User Education in the Humanities in U.S. Academic Libraries.* British Library Research and Development Reports. No. 5474. London: British Library, 1979.

Summarizes the author's visit to 24 academic libraries in the U.S. to study user education programs in the humanities. He found that most of the libraries give user instruction to freshman English courses. A variety of user instruction utilizing many different methods is also given to other courses. Coordinating and cooperating efforts are being stressed among the U.S. librarians offering library instruction.

Freeman, Michael S. "Published Study Guides: What They Say about Libraries." *Journal of Academic Librarianship* 5 (November, 1979), pp. 252–255.

The author examined and analyzed 16 published texts which are used in courses on reading and study skills in academic institutions for included information on libraries. It was found that these publications do not provide a sophisticated approach to library research and often neglect to recommend important reference tools in the area of indexes and abstracts. Also librarians are not recommended as having a major function in the students' information and research needs.

Freeman, Michael S. *Researching Historical Problems. An Introduction to Basic Resources.* ERIC Document Reproduction Service, 1979. ED 165 766.

This is the description of an individualized slide-tape instruction program to teach students how to research historical problems. The 79 slides cover research strategy, organization of information and collection of information.

Frost, William J. *College Library Instruction/College Instruction: A Review of the Literature.* ERIC Document Reproduction Service, 1979. ED 167 131.

This document presents a review of 64 items on library instruction research as related to college teaching in general. Discussion of behavioral objectives, transfer of knowledge, cognitive knowledge and retention and others are included.

Fudge, Lucretia L. "Individualized Instruction in Using the *Readers'*

Guide, Applying Aptitude Treatment Interaction." Ph.D. dissertation, University of Southern California, 1979.

The purpose of this study was the designing of a multi-media package to teach the use of the *Readers' Guide* to 7th graders. The results of the study indicate that students can be successful in learning this type of library skill through an individualized media method as well as through the traditional lecture method.

Gebhard, Patricia. *Library Research: A Beginning Text in Bibliographic Searching*. ERIC Document Reproduction Service, 1979. ED 167 134.

This manual was developed at the University of California -- Santa Barbara to teach search strategy for term paper research to students in a two-unit course. Assignments are designed to apply the taught information and to develop students' critical thinking and problem-solving skills.

Gebhard, Patricia and Barbara Silver. *Library Skills: A Self-Paced Workbook*. ERIC Document Reproduction Service, 1979. ED 167 133.

This is a self-paced programmed workbook for a one-unit course on library resources used at the University of California-- Santa Barbara for freshman students.

George, Mary W. and Mary Ann O'Donnell. "The Bibliography and Research Methods Course in American Departments of English." *Literary Research Newsletter* 4 (Winter, 1979), pp. 9--23.

The article summarizes the results of the survey of English departments described by Jones (see below). It was found that the research methods courses in English departments are an accepted part of the graduate curriculum but the courses vary greatly in time spent on actually teaching research methodology.

Glogoff, Stuart. "Using Statistical Tests to Evaluate Library Instruction Sessions." *Journal of Academic Librarianship* 4 (January, 1979), pp. 438--442.

Librarians at the Pennsylvania State University are evaluating their library instruction through objective testing methods using statistical tests -- the "t" confidence interval, analysis of variance and chi square. Such testing methods may have much value for other librarians interested in library instruction evaluation.

Guskin, Alan E. and others. "The Academic Library as a Teaching Library: A Role for the 1980s." *Library Trends* 28 (Fall, 1979), pp. 281--296.

Discusses how academic libraries could respond to the challenges of the next decade by becoming "teaching libraries" in the broadest sense. Such teaching libraries will have commitment to the academic community as well as the community at large. The teaching library model at the University of Wisconsin--Parkside is described in detail.

Hagerman, William L. "Computer Supplemented Instruction Using Batch Processed Delayed Reinforcement and Feedback Compared to Teacher Directed Discussion Following Interactive Mediated Instruction for Freshman College Library Orientation." Ph.D. dissertation, University of Nebraska--Lincoln, 1979.
    This study tried to determine the value of computer supplemented instruction following mediated instruction for library orientation to freshmen using a criterion, a non-criterion and an aptitude test. It was found that computer supplemented instruction can be effective as supplementary instruction and in the efficient utilization of students' and instructors' time. Also students' attitude toward this instruction was favorable.

Hardesty, Larry. *Bibliographic Instruction: Defining, Organizing and Promoting a Program*. ERIC Document Reproduction Service, 1979. ED 163 892.
    This paper discusses the organization of bibliographic instruction programs in academic institutions. Included are factors for consideration when planning innovative programs.

Hardesty, Larry and others. "Evaluating Library-Use Instruction." *College and Research Libraries* 40 (July, 1979), pp. 309--317.
    Author discusses need for library instruction evaluation to gain administrative and financial support. The assessment of library use instruction at DePauw University is described. The description of the development of a reliable evaluation instrument is included and a copy of the instrument is appended.

Jamieson, D.G. and I.A. Simpson. "Reader Instruction in the Health Sciences at Otago." *New Zealand Libraries* 41 (December, 1978), pp. 110--113.
    Discusses reader instruction at the medical and dental libraries at the University of Otago in Dunedin. The instruction consists of tours and subject-related lectures followed by exercises.

Jennerich, Elaine Z. and Bessie H. Smith. "A Bibliographic Instruction Program in Music." *College and Research Libraries* 40 (May, 1979), pp. 226--233.

Describes a course-integrated library instruction program for undergraduate music majors at Baylor University. Using a combination of lecture and worksheet method, good planning with the course instructor and evaluation has helped to make the instruction successful. The test and worksheet have been appended.

Jones, John B. "Introduction to the Surveys of the Bibliography and Research Methods Course." *Literary Research Newsletter* 4 (Winter, 1979), pp. 3--7.
Summarizes the planning of a survey of 108 English departments in the U.S. granting doctorates to find out what types of graduate level research methods courses are provided and to assess the course content.

Kennedy, James R. *Library Research Guide to Education*. Ann Arbor, MI: Pierian Press, 1979.
This book presents an illustrated search strategy and sources for the undergraduate education students. It is similar in format to the *Library Research Guide to Religion and Theology* by the same author and the *Library Research Guide to Biology* by Thomas Kirk. It covers the choice of topics, the card catalog, evaluation of books, current educational information, government documents, education reference books and the periodical indexes.

Kernaghan, John A. and others. "The Influences of Traditional Services on Library Use." *College and Research Libraries* 40 (May, 1979), pp. 214--239.
This study utilized 655 students in five medical schools to assess the relationship between user preferences, library characteristics and frequency of library use. Information-seeking behavior of medical students in this study was influenced by various factors – good collection, availability of current information, AV materials and library staff assistance. The latter includes library use instruction.

Kirkendall, Carolyn. *Improving Library Instruction: How to Teach and How to Evaluate*. Ann Arbor, MI: Pierian Press, 1979.
These papers were presented at the Eighth Annual Conference on Library Orientation for Academic Libraries held at Eastern Michigan University May 4--5, 1978. They include information on learning and motivation by I. Woronoff, instructional development by L. Hardesty, teaching librarians to teach in Britain by P. Fox, library instruction in the past and future by E. Holley, a panel on instructional methods and a panel evaluating instruc-

tional programs.

Kirkendall, Carolyn. "Library Instruction." *Journal of Academic Librarianship* 4 (January, 1979), pp. 444--445.
This column focuses on the state-of-the-art report on term paper clinics as a method of library use instruction. Librarians from Northern Illinois University, University of Maryland, Northeastern University, SUNY at Binghamton, University of Illinois and William Paterson College present their opinions.

Kirkendall, Carolyn. "Library Instruction: A Column of Opinion." *Journal of Academic Librarianship* 5 (March, 1979), pp. 28--29.
The question on how to obtain and maintain faculty co-operation for library instruction is answered by librarians from Bloomsburg State College, University of British Columbia, James Madison University, Penn State University and Normandale Community College.

Kirkendall, Carolyn. "Library Instruction: A Column of Opinion." *Journal of Academic Librarianship* 5 (May, 1979), pp. 86--87.
The question posed is whether or not library directors really believe that job applicants for reference positions should be experienced in library instruction. Four library directors from Providence College, David Lipscomb College, University of Richmond and Franklin and Marshall College offer their varied opinions.

Kirkendall, Carolyn. "Library Instruction: A Column of Opinion." *Journal of Academic Librarianship* 5 (September, 1979), pp. 222--223.
The issue concerning library instruction possibilities and/or difficulties at large research libraries is addressed by librarians from the University of Kentucky, Iowa State University, Northern Illinois University, University of Maryland, Pennsylvania State University and Ohio State University.

Kirkendall, Carolyn. "Library Instruction: A Column of Opinion." *Journal of Academic Librarianship* 5 (November, 1979), pp. 284--285.
This column addresses the concern of library instruction having reached a "plateau" because "the cutting edge of library use instruction has been dulled." Librarians from Suffolk University, University of Rochester, Columbia University, College of Charleston, Bucknell University, Herbert H. Lehman College and Oklahoma State University responded in the negative. Library

use instruction is more alive than ever and is generating continuous interest.

Kitchens, Philip H. "Engineers Meet the Library." *Journal of Academic Librarianship* 5 (November, 1979), pp. 277--282.

Course-integrated library instruction for engineering students at the University of Alabama is described by the author. The new program was carefully planned in cooperation with teaching faculty and has been successful. Continuing attention to improving objectives, student motivation, library materials and evaluation of the program promise to keep this program a success.

Koyama, Janice. *LIP Notes: A Syllabus for the Library Instruction Program, University Library, California State University, Long Beach*. ERIC Document Reproduction Service, 1979. ED 171 292.

This is a working syllabus for classroom use and an outline for lecture presentations by librarians on library instruction. It includes questions asked most frequencly at reference desks, instruction in the selection and evaluation of reference sources and search strategy.

Lester, Ray. "Why Educate the Library User?" *Aslib Proceedings* 31 (August, 1979), pp. 366--380.

The author of this paper presented at an Aslib meeting discusses the nature of information in relationship to the user based on Wilson's *Public Knowledge, Private Ignorance*. He argues that the formal courses in library user education taught especially in higher education are misconceived and should be abolished. He advocates instead that library user education should be an integral part of academic coursework, should be given by subject teachers and should communicate the importance of libraries in the area of information and communication.

Library Service Enhancement Program 1976–1977. Presbyterian College Library. ERIC Document Reproduction Service, 1979. ED 174 260.

This document contains program proposal, interim and final reports of a program for bibliographic instruction at Presbyterian College. The program is based on close cooperation between faculty and librarians.

Library Service Enhancement Program. Tusculum College. Final Report: July 1, 1977--June 30, 1978. ERIC Document Reproduction Service, 1979. ED 174 261.

Provides the final report on Tusculum College's library instruction program designed to ensure bibliographic competency of all graduating sociology and social services majors.

Lindsey, Jonathan. "The Librarian: An Educator in the Collegiate Library." *North Carolina Libraries* 32 (Winter, 1979), pp. 5--10.

The author discusses role models for college librarians, the various functions college librarians must perform, the rank and status of college librarians and their educating role on campus.

Lolley, John L. and Ruth Watkins. "The Use of Audio-Visuals in Developing Favorable Attitudes toward Library Instruction." *Educational Technology* (September, 1979), pp. 56--58.

Discusses pros and cons of AV materials in library use instruction. One of the reasons for the failure of AV programs in library instruction has been that the "why" of library instruction has been ignored. They also lack motivational factors for students. The authors discuss how this can be changed by incorporating factors for students' attitude change toward library skills into the AV materials.

Malley, Ian. *User Education in Academic Libraries*. Papers presented at a seminar at University of Strathclyde on November 20, 1978. INFUSE Supplement No. 5. Loughborough, Leicestershire, 1979.

Mayes, P.B. *Readability of User Education Materials*. British Library Research and Development Reports No. 5484. London: British Library, 1979.

The author tested various library guides for their readability by applying six readability formulas (Coleman, Elley, Bormuth, Flesh R.E., Dale-Chall, Fog Index). The readability of these guides was tested with 45 undergraduate students. The author found that the Coleman Ref. 1 test is most simple and quick to use.

Meyer, Wayne. "The Three Phases of Bibliographic Instruction." *Wisconsin Library Bulletin* 75 (March--April, 1979). pp. 63--65.

The author discusses three phases in course-related library instruction in academic institutions -- innovation, program involvement, marketing and management.

Morris, Jacqueline M. and Donald F. Webster. *Developing Objectives for Library Instruction*. ERIC Document Reproduction Service, 1979. ED 171 257.

Description of a workshop on developing objectives for library instruction programs. Includes discussion of the necessity of program planning, strategies for planning specific library instruction programs and frequent problems within library instruction programs.

Morton, Bruce. "Beyond Orientation: The Library as Place of Education and the Librarian as Educator." *Improving College and University Teaching* 27 (Fall, 1979), pp. 161--163.

The author discusses the librarian's instructional role in the academic institution. Students should not just be oriented to the library but should receive meaningful education in the use of library resources through cooperation with classroom instructors.

Murray, Carolyn K. "Teaching the COM Microcatalogue." *RQ* 18 (Fall, 1979), pp. 52--57.

The article discusses the University of Toronto Library's experience with educating users and staff in the use of the COM microcatalog. Six different methods were used. The most effective one was a flip chart. This project has been most beneficial to the over-all library instruction program.

Olivetti, L. James. "Utilizing Natural Structure of the Research Literature in Psychology as a Model for Bibliographic Instruction." *Behavioral and Social Sciences Librarian* 1 (Fall, 1979), pp. 43--46.

This article describes an alternative to the search strategy method of library use instruction in psychology. The particular method described uses Festinger's theory of cognitive dissonance to teach analysis of the natural structure of the research literature.

Organizing and Managing a Library Instruction Program: Checklists. Prepared by the ALA ACRL Bibliographic Instruction Section, Continuing Education Committee for the Preconference at Southern Methodist University, Dallas, TX, 1979.

The 12 checklists included in this booklet were prepared to help librarians implement, initiate and/or improve library instruction programs. The topics covered by the checklists are: need assessment, assessment of faculty interest, program administration, development of objectives, instructional methods, development of instructional materials, preparing librarians to teach, evaluation, gaining of collegial and institutional support.

Paterson, Ellen P. "How Effective Is Library Instruction?" *RQ* 18 (Summer, 1979), pp. 376--377.

The author discusses use of a pre-test on library knowledge with biology and health educaticn students at SUNY -- Cortland. Contrary to the author's expectation very mixed test results occurred.

Patterson, Thomas H. *Political Studies Library Skills Test*. ERIC Document Reproduction Service, 1979. ED 160 116.

This library skills test will assess students' knowledge and ability to use political studies library resources. It contains three sections, a matching and completion questions part, multiple choice questions and true--false questions. No answer key is provided.

Pearson, Lennart. "What Has the Library Done for You Lately?" *Improving College and University Teaching* 26 (Fall, 1978), pp. 219--221.

The author discusses the need to teach students bibliographic skills by building them into the college curriculum. Various ways are suggested to classroom teachers to seek cooperation from their librarians. Among some of the suggestions is one to involve librarians in curricular planning and decision-making.

Pernacciaro, Samuel J. and Carla J. Stoffle. "Introducing Students to Library Source Materials." *News for Teachers of Political Science* 20 (Winter, 1979), pp. 15--16.

The authors discuss the need for teaching students majoring in political science effective information gathering skills in that discipline. A self-paced library research manual in political science has been developed by the authors to teach students such skills. The organization of the manual, its use and evaluation are also discussed.

Phillips, Linda L. and E.A. Raup. "Comparing Methods for Teaching Use of Periodical Indexes." *Journal of Academic Librarianship* 4 (January, 1979), pp. 420--423.

This article discusses a comparative study of the lecture and programmed method of library instruction in use of periodical literature. Various testing methods were used. It was found that both teaching methods have merit.

Phipps, Shelley and Ruth Dickstein. "The Library Skills Program at the University of Arizona: Testing, Evaluation and Critique." *Journal of Academic Librarianship* 5 (September, 1979), pp. 205--214.

The article summarizes the library skills program and its

evaluation at the University of Arizona. An individualized workbook adapted from M. Dudley's was used to teach library skills within English composition courses. Pre- and posttests were used to measure the effect of the workbooks in changing students' awareness of library resources and services. It was found that the workbooks brought about some library skills learning especially in the area of teaching students the variety of information available in various reference books. Some skills like use and interpretation of information in journal indexes were not taught well. Also assignments must be tailored to the objectives of the text to be successful.

Rader, Hannelore B. *An Assessment of Ten Academic Library Instruction Programs in the United States and Canada.* ERIC Document Reproduction Service, 1979. ED 171 276.

This report summarizes ten existing academic library instruction programs in the U.S. and Canada. Investigated were administrative and staff support, instructional methods and materials. Objectives, statistical records and program evaluations were found to be important organizational factors.

Ready, Sandra K. *Development of a Self-Instructional Course for Library Orientation at Mankato State University.* ERIC Document Reproduction Service, 1979. ED 169 894.

This study describes the development of a self-instructional program for basic library instruction at Mankato State University. The materials can be used as self-instructional units and for large group presentations. Included are scripts for slide-tape presentations.

Renford, Beverly L. *Library Resources: A Self-Paced Workbook.* ERIC Document Reproduction Service, 1979. ED 163 956.

This workbook produced at Pennsylvania State University library is designed to teach undergraduate students basic library skills on an individualized and independent basis.

Rice, Sheila. *Workbook for the Introduction to the Library.* ERIC Document Reproduction Service, 1979. ED 163 953.

This workbook was produced at the University of Michigan Undergraduate Library for freshman students to learn basic library skills.

Rockman, Ilene F. *Library Instruction to EOP Students: A Case Study.* ERIC Documents Reproduction Service, 1979. ED 174 211.

Discusses a ten-week one-credit library skills course for Educational Opportunity Program students at California Polytechnic State University at San Luis Obispo. The course is part of these students' core curriculum which stresses communication skills.

Schildhauer, Carole. *Bibliographic Instruction I: Development of an Instructional Program*. ERIC Document Reproduction Service, 1979. ED 174 250.

Provides a discussion of the development of an integrated library instruction package including guidelines for choice of topic, audience definition, instructional objectives, script writing and program evaluation.

Shapiro, Beth and Richard C. Hill. 'Teaching Sociology Graduate Students Bibliographic Methods for Document Research." *Journal of Academic Librarianship* 5 (May, 1979), pp. 75--78.

The article describes a graduate seminar for credit for sociology students on bibliography methods for documents research. The seminar was organized around problem definitions, strategy of the literature search, techniques of an effective search process and critical evaluation of results. This proved a very positive experience and opened up more possibilities for future library-faculty cooperation at Michigan State University.

Stebelman, Scott. "Self-Paced Tours at UN-L." *Nebraska Library Association Quarterly* 9 (Winter, 1978), pp. 23--25.

Describes the use of self-paced workbooks to orient students to the library and the use of the card catalog and the *Readers' Guide* at the University of Nebraska--Lincoln through the English composition course. Librarians introduce the packets and grade them.

State-of-the-Art of Academic Library Instruction. 1977 Update. ERIC Document Reproduction Service, 1979. ED 171 272.

Included are ten papers updating various areas of academic library instruction. Covered are library tours, point-of-use library instruction, credit courses, term paper clinics, AV materials in library instruction and library school courses to prepare future librarians for library instruction.

Stockard, Joan. *A Directory of Bibliographic Instruction Programs in New England Academic Libraries*. ERIC Document Reproduction Service, 1979. ED 171 259.

This is a computer-produced directory listing library instruction programs in New England academic libraries. The information is based on collected questionnaires.

Stoffle, Carla and Simon Carter. *Materials and Methods for History Research*. New York: Neal-Schuman, 1979.
This is the first in the series of discipline-oriented workbooks developed by C. Stoffle and other staff at the University of Wisconsin--Parkside. It is intended to teach students information search strategies in the area of history, either through independent study or through course-related instruction. Included in the library edition are a workbook and an instructor's manual.

Stoffle, Carla and others. *Materials and Methods for Political Science Research*. New York: Neal-Schuman, 1979.
This is the second in the series of discipline-oriented workbooks developed by C. Stoffle and the staff at University of Wisconsin--Parkside. It is designed to teach students search strategies in the area of political science. The library edition includes the student workbook and the instructor's manual.

Suprenant, Thomas. "A Comparison of Lecture and Programmed Instruction in the Teaching of Basic Catalog Card and Bibliographic Index Information." Ph.D. dissertation, University of Wisconsin--Madison, 1979.
This study used freshmen in four academic institutions in the Midwest to compare the lecture and programmed instruction methods in teaching use of the card catalog and periodical indexes. The Solomon Four Group Experimental Design was used for the comparison. Results were not useful for the conceptual level of learning. It was concluded that learning can be divided into levels and can then be measured effectively. Indications are that programmed instruction is better than lecturing for teaching use of card catalog and indexes.

The Taming of the Dinosaur: A Key to Library Resources. Unit I . . . The Card Catalog: Locating Books. ERIC Document Reproduction Service, 1979. ED 163 923.
This is an individualized self-instruction unit for students at the University of Kentucky to familiarize them with the use of the card catalog. Questions are provided for the students to review the learned information.

The Taming of the Dinosaur: A Key to Library Resources: Unit 2 . . . Sources of Current Information: Locating Periodical and Newspaper Articles. ERIC Document Reproduction Service, 1979. ED 163 924.

135

This self-instruction unit at the library of the University of Kentucky deals with teaching students how to find current information and how to use indexes.

The Taming of the Dinosaur: A Key to Library Resources: Unit 3. . . Reference Material: Library Search Strategy. ERIC Document Reproduction Service, 1979. ED 163 925.

This unit on library skills for students at the University of Kentucky library deals with reference materials and library search strategy. A flow chart presentation of search strategies is also included.

"Termpapers without Tears." *Unabashed Librarian* 31 (1979), pp. 6--8.

Describes how to prepare for and do a term paper. Gives many practical suggestions.

Tippet, Harriet. "Evaluating the Lawrence University Program." *Wisconsin Library Bulletin* 75 (March-April, 1979), p. 62.

Provides a short assessment of the library instruction program at Lawrence University. States that there is a need for it. There is also a need for assessing students' library skills before and after instruction.

Todd, Joanna. "Bibliographic Instruction in the Hugh Stephens Library." *Show-Me Libraries* 30 (June, 1979), pp. 34--35.

Describes the library instruction program at Stephens College in Missouri. The program utilizes librarians as liaison with academic departments to build library-faculty cooperation and course-related library instruction.

Volker, Joyce. "AV and Reader Education." *Australian Academic and Research Libraries* 10 (June, 1979), pp. 120--121.

This is a report of a seminar to study educational and technical criteria in planning AV materials for user education.

Williams, Mitsuko and Elisabeth B. Davis. "Evaluation of PLATO Library Instructional Lessons." *Journal of Academic Librarianship* 5 (March, 1979), pp. 14--19.

The article discusses library instruction to biology students using PLATO in a computer assisted instruction at the University of Illinois at Urbana. An evaluation of the program has shown that students prefer this method because of the one-to-one instruction. Individualized assistance from librarians is the next preference.

136

Wilson, Pauline. "Librarians as Teachers: The Study of an Organization Fiction." *Library Quarterly* 49 (January, 1979), pp. 146--162.

The author defines organization fiction and applies it to librarianship. Librarians as teachers is the organization fiction discussed in the article. Reasons for this fiction are provided and the harmful effect of this fiction upon librarians' professional self-image is explained.

Wood, Richard J. *A Computer-Assisted Instruction Program on How to Use a Library Card Catalog: Description, Program and Evaluation.* ERIC Document Reproduction Service, 1979. ED 167 156.

Describes a BASIC computer program at Slippery Rock State College library to teach students the use of the card catalog. A manual was developed in conjunction with the program.

Yerburgh, Mark R. "The Utilization of Academic Librarians as Classroom Teachers: Some Brief Observations." *Academe* (November, 1979), pp. 441--443.

The author discusses how academic librarians can become involved in the teaching process on campus. Librarians possess bibliographic and often subject skills, the combination of these could make for some very effective teaching. Through careful institutional planning and faculty-librarian cooperation the librarians could become a rich resource for campus teaching and not a threat to the faculty.

PUBLIC LIBRARIES

Frey, Amy L. and Saul Spigel. "Educating Adult Users in the Public Library." *Library Journal* 104 (April 15, 1979), pp. 894--896.

The authors describe how they tried to help public library users cope with finding information. They have developed a "reference newsletter" which lists new annotated reference books and pathfinders for different subjects. They also planned and held a series of reference workshops.

Hendley, Margaret. "The Librarian as Teacher: Research Skills for Library Patrons at Kitchener Public Library." *Ontario Library Review* 63 (March, 1979), pp. 45--48.

Discusses how at Kitchener Public Library credit and free courses are offered by two local universities and how this generated a need for library instruction to patrons. The public library now offers research skills workshops on a regular basis. The publicity for this workshop and the holding of the workshop are described.

Irving, Anne. "New Directions for Libraries." *Library Association Record* 81 (April, 1979), p. 179+.
The author discusses librarians' responsibility in adult education through teaching the finding of information and reading strategies to adult learners.

Winslow, Theresa. "Homework Helpers." *New Jersey Libraries* 12 (September, 1979), pp. 16–17.
The Vineland Public Library started a project called "Homework Helpers" to aid students who come to the library after school and need to find information. These students also need someone to help them clarify assignments. Members of the teacher sorority Alpha Delta Kappa receive library instruction training and are then available to help students.

Zahorski, Marijean A. "Programs Can Instruct." *Wisconsin Library Bulletin* 75 (March–April, 1979), pp 53–54.
The article discusses how the Brown County Library in Wisconsin reaches out to the community through programs and library instruction.

SCHOOL LIBRARIES

Anderson, Robert. "Academic Survival Skills." *Wisconsin Library Bulletin* 75 (March–April), 1979. p. 69.
Discusses a new approach to library orientation in the Reuther Alternative High School in Kenosha, Wisconsin. It is in the format of a nine-week course for English credit to acquaint students with library information-seeking skills and life-long learning skills.

Anderson, Pauline. "What's Going On in Independent Schools." *School Library Journal* 26 (November, 1979), pp. 33–41.
The National Association of Independent Schools at their March, 1979 conference discussed developments in independent schools libraries. Among many concerns was the library instruction issue and a BLISS (Bibliographic and Library Instruction in Secondary Schools) clearinghouse for instructional materials used in independent school libraries was established at the Andrew Mellon Library, Choate Rosemary Hall in Wallingford, CT.

Bell, Irene W. and Jeanne E. Wieckert. *Basic Media Skills Through*

Games. Littleton, CO: Libraries Unlimited, 1979.

This manual offers to teach students library skills including how to locate materials, how to use the card catalog, reference books and audiovisual equipment. Among the many games provided for elementary school students are quite a few which can be made by older students and library aides out of inexpensive materials. Included are 74 games, a chart of the progression of IMC skills and a list of reference books used in the games.

Bernstein, Mae and others. *Action and Interaction: A Secondary Library Media Program.* ERIC Document Reproduction Service, 1979. ED 160 111.

This is a curriculum guide for librarians and classroom teachers to instruct secondary students in library skills. Objectives, activities, a glossary of library terms and a bibliography are included.

Bertrand, Lynda and Jeanne Klatt. "Mutant Melvil Ameliorates Media Skills." *Wisconsin Library Bulletin* 75 (March--April, 1979), pp. 71--73.

The authors discuss a creative media skills program for elementary students.

Biggs, Mary. "Forward to Basics in Library Instruction." *School Library Journal* 25 (May, 1979), p. 44.

The author bemoans the fact that high school graduates in general lack library skills and that at this point it is up to academic librarians to teach them these skills. It is advocated that school librarians cooperate with teachers to provide basic skills in library know-how just like basic skills are now taught in reading, writing and mathematics.

Brake, Terrence. "The Need to Know: Teaching the Importance and Use of Information at School." *Education Libraries Bulletin* 22 (1979), pp. 38--51.

Christine, E.R. "Multimedia Library Skills for Today's Child: A Suggested Sequence." *CMLEA Journal* 1 (Winter, 1978), pp. 22--27.

"College Library Prep." *School Library Journal* 26 (October, 1979), pp. 67--68.

Several letters from school librarians to the editor comment on Mary Biggs' "Forward to Basics in Library Instruction" (see above). Many of the reasons for lack of library skills are pointed out.

"Comments." *Catholic Library World* 50 (March, 1979), pp. 342--345.

Twelve comments on the article describing pathfinders by Stanton are printed lauding them as a most practical aid to library instruction especially in schools.

Doyle, Carol M. "Media for Library Skills Instruction." *Previews* 7 (February, 1979), pp. 2--8.

The author discusses criteria for children's need to become skilled library/media center users. A program based on continuous levels of instruction is described. An extensive list of library instruction materials is appended.

Duryee, Joan and Dorothy Stoutjeschyk. "Developing a K--6 Media Center Skills Curriculum." *Media Spectrum* 6 (1979), p. 19+.

Describes the media center skills curriculum developed in 1978/79 by elementary school media specialists in the South Redford School District. The objective was to help elementary school students in K--6 master seven skills areas coordinated with the classroom curriculum. Specific instructional methods and materials for each level are provided.

Elementary Media Curriculum for Teachers and Media Specialists. ERIC Document Reproduction Service, 1979. ED 169 041.

Provides guidelines for the development of a library skills curriculum for elementary school students. Concentrates on the teaching of use of AV equipment. Activities and evaluation criteria are also given.

Elliott, Anna B. "Show Them with Pictures." *Momentum* 10 (February, 1979), p. 17.

Describes the making of a chart to teach Dewey Decimal codes and to help young children become familiar with the library.

Foth, Cindy. "Middle School Instruction at All Levels." *Nebraska Library Association Quarterly* 9 (Winter, 1978), p. 16.

Describes the library instruction program at C.L. Jones Middle School in Minden, Nebraska to fourth, fifth and sixth graders. Workbooks are used.

Freeman, Doria L. and others. *Action and Interaction: An Elementary Library Media Program.* ERIC Document Reproduction Service, 1979. ED 161 437.

This is a curriculum guide to teach library skills to elementary students and features learning activities to reinforce media skills.

Gibson, Mary J. and MIldred Kaczmarek. *Finding Information in the Library: A Guide to Reference Sources for Rochelle High School Students.* 2d ed. ERIC Document Reproduction Service, 1979. ED 161 460.

This manual was designed for high school students to teach them library research. It includes information on library sources usually taught to freshmen in college. Subject reference sources are also covered for advanced research in the social sciences, humanities and sciences.

Gibson, Mary J. and Mildred Kaczmarek. *Student Activity Workbook for Use with Finding Information in the Library.* ERIC Document Reproduction Service, 1979. ED 161 461.

This is designed for freshmen high school students to be used with the document above to learn library skills. For each exercise students have to supply written answers.

Grooters, Lyle E. "Library Media Skills Guide." *Wisconsin Library Bulletin* 75 (March--April, 1979), p. 66.

Discusses the development of a guide for the teaching of media skills in Wisconsin school libraries by the Wisconsin School Library Media Association. This guide emphasizes the integration of media skills into all curriculum areas and the sharing of instruction of these skills by teachers and librarians.

Herring, James. "Where's 635?" *New Library World* 80 (January, 1979), pp. 7--9.

The author discusses the need for library skills instruction to begin in elementary school and the necessity of having library skills training as part of a teacher preparation curriculum.

Knepel, Nancy P. "Mix Skills with Fun." *Wisconsin Library Bulletin* 75 (March--April, 1979), pp. 57--58.

Talks about teaching library skills to juveniles in a correctional institution to prepare them for future library use.

Lansner, Helen. "Special Report: Making the Very Best of a Bad Thing." *Wilson Library Bulletin* 53 (February, 1979), pp. 456--457.

This report discusses the teaching of reference/media skills to high school students in New York City through a regular credit course. Motivation of the students and meaningful projects for them are also discussed.

Lewsey, Elizabeth. "Complaints from a Librarian." *Art and Craft in*

Education 253 (February, 1979), p. 3.

This short article addresses teachers and encourages them to cooperate with public librarians for their own information and for the educational benefits of all their students.

Miller, Robert E. "Teaching Skills in the Retrieval and Utilization of Materials and Equipment for Students and Faculty." *Catholic Library World* 50 (March, 1979), pp. 327--329.

The article discusses the importance of providing materials and support to enrich the instructional program and to teach students library skills in elementary and secondary schools. Close communication with students and faculty is advocated and practical advice for that is given.

Penn, Phyllis. "Children Learn Library Use." *Wisconsin Library Bulletin* 75 (March--April, 1979), pp 55--56.

Discusses a K--8 library skills program developed by the Marathon County public library in Wisconsin. This is offered in cooperation with local teachers.

Peterson, Donna. "Commitment to Skills. Basis of Junior High Plan." *Nebraska Library Association Quarterly* 9 (Winter, 1978), pp. 17--18.

The author describes the library skills program for seventh, eighth and ninth graders at Lefter Junior High School in Lincoln, Nebraska. Various instructional methods and materials are utilized.

Probasco, Carol. "Magic Circle . . . Hob of Learning." *Nebraska Library Association Quarterly* 9 (Winter, 1978), pp. 10--12.

Discusses a media skills program for students at Maude Rousseau Elementary School in Lincoln, Nebraska based on continuous levels of instruction.

Sampson, Marilyn. "Library Appreciation Learned Along with Library Skills." *Nebraska Library Association Quarterly* 9 (Winter, 1978), pp. 20--21.

Discusses library skills teaching from the second to the eighth grade at Clay Center Public Schools in Nebraska. Also taught are literary appreciation skills through units on the Newbery Award books.

Sawin, Marjorie. "High School Program Aimed toward Lifelong Skills." *Nebraska Library Association Quarterly* 9 (Winter, 1978), pp. 18--22.

Describes the library instruction program at Lincoln High School in Nebraska. The program is administered in close co-operation with English teachers and utilizing English coursework. Special emphasis is given to life-long learning skills with a view to using libraries.

Schomberg, J. and C. Erdahl. "Elementary Grade Students Learn to Operate AV Equipment. A Case Study of a Program that Works." *Preview* 8 (November, 1979), pp. 2--4.

Shapiro, Lillian L. *Teaching Yourself in Libraries: A Guide to the High School Media Center and Other Libraries.* New York: Wilson, 1978.
This book is intended as a self-study manual for high school students and features an unusual approach in teaching reference sources. The author calls it "a sort of traveler's aid for young people" to learn about the library independently through curriculum-oriented units. Sample test questions are included at the end of each chapter.

Smith, Jane B. *Library Skills for Primary Grades.* ERIC Document Reproduction Service, 1979. ED 174 262.
Describes a field-tested library skills program for second and third graders. Student worksheets and student activities are included.

Spirt, Diana L. *Library/Media Manual.* New York: Wilson, 1979.

Stanton, Vida C. "Roadmaps through Information Sources." *Catholic Library World* 50 (March, 1979), p. 340.
The author discusses the use of guides to subject areas or pathfinders in school libraries. She points out that even though the preparation of these guides may be time-consuming, the benefits derived from their use by students may be well worth the effort.

Study Skills Related to Library Use: A K--12 Curriculum Guide for Teachers and Librarians. ERIC Document Reproduction Service, 1979. ED 169 906.
This guide identifies the library skills for students in K--12 and provides a sequential outline of skills to teach. Objectives, activities, resources and evaluation methods are given.

Tassia, Margaret. "It's Not Just a Game." *School Library Journal* 25 (March, 1979), pp. 105--107.
Games to teach library skills to disinterested students are

143

discussed here. Details are provided to develop games according to certain themes which will arouse student interest.

Turner, Phillip M. and Nina N. Martin. " Instructional Development at the K--12 Level: Attitudes and Activities." *Southeastern Librarian* 29 (Spring, 1979), pp. 15–18.
Summarizes a study to ascertain the involvement of media specialists (K--12) in instructional development activities. The study involved 67 percent of 300 schools in Alabama during 1977–78. It was found that among the seven most frequent activities of these media specialists was the provision of instruction in use of materials and equipment but among the seven least frequently performed tasks was the participation in curriculum development.

Wellner, Henry J. "Dewey Can Be Fun." *Wisconsin Library Bulletin* 75 (March--April, 1979), pp. 67–69.
The Kenosha school system has an extensive K--12 library skills program. Recently they have developed new instructional materials including videotapes and games to teach the Dewey Decimal system.

Warren, Rayda and Joanna Link. "A High School Library Skills Program that Works." *Media Spectrum* 5 (1979), p. 17.
Describes a library instruction program at John Glenn High School. The library skills unit is taught in the tenth grade English class by media specialists. Pre- and posttests are given.

Wilsher, Gary S. *For a Higher Interest Rate -- Sign the Bottom Line.* ERIC Document Reproduction Service, 1979. ED 174 204.
Describes a library skills program for elementary schools utilizing specific objectives and teacher-librarian contracts. Includes behavioral objectives contracts for students in K--5.

SPECIAL LIBRARIES AND GROUPS

Allen, Nancy. "Instruction to Library Users." In *Film Study Collections: A Guide to Their Development and Use.* New York: Ungar, 1979, pp. 106--112.
This chapter discusses the importance and how-to of library use instruction in the area of film study. A sample library lecture is presented.

Allen, Stephanie N. and others. "The Implementation of a Large Scale Self-Instructional Course in Medical Information Resources." *Bulletin of the Medical Library Association* 67 (1979), pp. 302–307.

Antony, A. *Guide to Basic Information Sources in Chemistry*. New York: Jeffrey Norton, 1979.

This is an annotated listing of chemistry sources (indexes, bibliographies, dictionaries) intended for the use of chemistry students but it is not a guide to the use of the literature or the use of abstracting services.

Beleu, S. *Microforms: An Introduction to the Department of Energy Collection, Early English Books Collection and the Human Relations Area Files of the University of Oklahoma*. ERIC Document Reproduction Service, 1979. ED 165 768.

Included are three guides which provide instructions in the use of specific indexes to find items in each collection. Step-by-step directions are used to take users from topic to relevant information.

Cohen, Diana B. "User Guide to the Publications and Documentation of the International Labour Office." *Government Publications Review* 6 (1979), pp. 157–159.

This is an annotated bibliography on publications and documentation from the International Labour Office.

Hatt, F. "Library Instruction, Individualized Learning and Independent Learning." *Art Library Journal* 3 (Winter, 1978), pp. 5–16.

Metcalf, Mary J. "Helping Hearing Impaired Students." *School Library Journal* 25 (January, 1979), pp. 27–29.

Author discusses problems with teaching hearing-impaired children to read and to use libraries. A description of a K–8 library skills curriculum is provided using visual materials with every lesson. Problems with card catalogs are pointed out and changes are suggested.

Meyers, Sister Edna M. "Teaching Library Skills to Deaf Children." *Catholic Library World* 51 (September, 1979), pp. 58–60.

The author advocates that library skills instruction should begin with very young children and story telling and continue to more sophisticated levels each year. In order to be effective library instruction must have meaning for the children, it should be taught when needed. Eventually the children learn to be independent library users. The described program is especially aimed at deaf children.

Montemayor, Aurelio M. and Garry Stillman. *Integrating Library Skills Instruction into the Bilingual Bicultural Classrooms or Preventing LESA Future Shock.* ERIC Document Reproduction Service, 1979. ED 165 462.

Suggests that library skills instruction should be incorporated into bilingual, bicultural programs because students with limited English speaking ability have a great need for current information skills. It is advocated that teaching of library skills should become integrated with the teaching of other communication skills.

Pesaitis, Patricia and Judith A. Hays. *Library Resources in Gerontology: Periodicals, Indexes and Abstracts. University Gerontology Center Information Report No. 2.* ERIC Document Reproduction Service, 1979. ED 168 511.

This guide discusses periodicals, indexes and abstracting services in the area of gerontology and geriatrics available at Wichita State University. Information on how to use these sources and short review exercises are provided.

Reference Resources for Research and Continuing Education in Nursing. ERIC Document Reproduction Service, 1979. ED 169 798.

The three papers included here address concerns like what are library resources and how can they be used in nursing, what skills in library resources should nursing students have, and the significance of literature searching.

Ridgeway, Patricia M. "Orientation/Instruction Round-Up." *South Carolina Librarian* 23 (Spring, 1979), pp. 6–7.

Discusses library orientation and instruction for blind users. Library guides in braille and on audiotape are being used in some academic libraries. Also discussed are audiovisual materials.

Shaaban, Marian. "Examination of Published and Unpublished Manuals and Handouts on United Nations Documentation." *Government Publications Review* 6 (1979), pp. 151–156.

This is an annotated bibliography of instructional manuals and handouts for users of United Nations documents and publications of the European communities. Included are commercially published and library-prepared materials.

Stapleton, Diana L. *Student Manual.* ERIC Document Reproduction Service, 1979. ED 168 528.

This manual was designed for student assistants in government documents section of the Eastern Kentucky University Library. It covers policy, procedures and use of major document reference sources.

Sullivan, Catherine. "Survey of In-House User Education in Special Libraries." *Aslib Proceedings* 31 (July, 1979), pp. 322–333.
This is report of a survey of user education in 698 special libraries in the United Kingdom sponsored by the British Library Research and Development Department. It was found that user education in special libraries is quite varied depending on the type of special library -- government, industry, science. User instruction is often useful for the promotion of services.

A User's Guide to the Jones Microtext Center. ERIC Document Reproduction Service, 1979. ED 165 767.
This guide to the Jones Microtext Center at Dartmouth College includes information on how to locate and use items in that collection. Description of the Center's holdings and services are also given.

White, Donald J. "Orientation Course Aids Staff on the Job." *Canadian Library Journal* 36 (February--April, 1979), pp. 17--20.
The article discusses library use instruction courses for secretaries, administrative assistants, laboratory, teaching and research assistants at the University of Victoria. It was found that there is much interest for such a course, that it should be taught to a small group, that practical work should be incorporated into the course and that the needs of the users should be assessed before the instruction is provided.

ALL LEVELS

Cipolla, Katharine G. *Bibliographic Instruction II: Production of an Instructional Program in a Non-Print Medium.* ERIC Document Reproduction Service, 1979. ED 174 251.
This paper discusses the use of non-print media in library instruction. The use of audio-tape, slide-tape, videotape and film is suggested for bibliographic instruction. Production information and possible problems are described.

Clark, Daphne. "Helping Librarians to Help Their Users." *Unesco Bulletin for Libraries* 32 (November, 1978), pp. 363--374.
The author discusses various ways in which librarians interested in providing library use instruction may get help. Literature

searches, professional organizations, conferences, demonstration projects, courses, manuals, prepared teaching materials, cooperative production of materials, and consultants are described.

Clark, Daphne. "Self-Instruction of Library Users." *ISG News* 12 (August, 1979), pp. 2–4.

Czisny, Julie. "Evaluating Skills Programs." *Wisconsin Library Bulletin* 75 (March–April, 1979), pp. 59–61.
The author discusses the importance of evaluating library use instruction and explains various types of possible evaluative methods.

Elkins, Elizabeth A. and Judith A. Byman. *Developing Printed Material for Library Instruction*. ERIC Document Reproduction Service, 1979. ED 171 258.
This is a packet of instructional materials for librarians interested in developing written materials for library instruction programs. The packet's objectives are to enable the librarian to become familiar with rationale for effective printed instructional materials, to be able to develop such materials and to identify appropriate materials for specific learning activities in library instruction.

Gavryck, Jacquelyn and Ruth Peabody. "Shaping the Library's In-House Publications Policy." *Wilson Library Bulletin* 54 (December, 1979), pp. 230–235.
The article covers several topics to include in a policy statement for library in-house publications (guides, bibliographies, point-of-use instruction and others). The topics which should be covered are types of publications, name of responsible unit, intended audience, updating provisions, support staff sources, cataloguing and copyright information and budgeting and administrative details.

Katz, William A. *Your Library: A Reference Guide*. New York: Holt, 1979.
This manual is directed toward students or beginning library users. The book is divided into two sections. The first section is on how to use a library and discusses librarians and reference sources. The second section is a key to library sources in the various subject areas. A title and a subject index are included.

Livingston, Barbara. "Special Report. N.Y. Graphics Seminar: Signs for Better Access." *Library Journal* 104 (February 1, 1979), pp. 343–344.

This report summarizes a "graphics in libraries" seminar where the functions of a sign system were defined as instructing, orienting and directing library users. Also discussed were color, placement, shape and materials of signs.

Lockwood, Deborah. *Library Instruction. A Bibliography*. Westport, CT: Greenwood Press, 1979.

This annotated bibliography covers materials written only in English, covers the period before 1970 only selectively and the period after 1970 comprehensively. Omitted have been materials intended for direct use of patrons on library use, e.g., workbooks. The bibliography is arranged by general philosophy, types of libraries, teaching methods and includes a name index.

Malley, Ian. *Current Research and Development Projects in User Education in the United Kingdom*. Papers presented at a conference held at Loughborough University of Technology on March 22, 1979. INFUSE Supplement No. 4, Loughborough, Leicestershire, UK, 1979.

Pollet, Dorothy. "Signs Are for People." *South Carolina Librarian* 23 (Fall, 1979), pp. 2–7.

This is a summary of a presentation at the Signage Workshop held in Columbia, SC on April 19, 1979. It discusses behavior in libraries, cognitive maps, components and characteristics of signage systems and other related special needs.

Prince, William and others. *List of Library Instruction Clearinghouses, Directories and Newsletters and Results of the Clearinghouse Questionnaires*. ERIC Document Reproduction Service, 1979. ED 165 762.

This resource list on library instruction clearinghouses, their publications and contact persons is intended to provide librarians interested and involved in library instruction with pertinent information.

Sign Systems for Libraries: Solving the Wayfinding Problem. Comp. and ed. by D. Pollet and Peter C. Haskell. New York: Bowker, 1979.

This book features a collection of writings about signage and graphics, especially as applied to all types of libraries. Several of the writings focus on signage as a means of user orientation and guidance to information. Many illustrations and a lengthy, annotated bibliography are included.

Tocatlan, Jacques. "Training Information Users. Programmes, Problems, Prospects." *Unesco Bulletin for Libraries* 32 (November-December, 1978), pp. 355--362.

This article presents a survey of *Unesco* and other international programs concerned with library instruction. Users are defined by groups and their information needs and information seeking behaviors are explained. Also discussed are national information policies and user training programs.

Wood, Vivian. "New Jersey Clearinghouse." *New Jersey Libraries* 12 (April, 1979), pp. 13--14.

Discusses the establishment of a clearinghouse for library instruction information in all types of libraries at Rutgers University's Graduate School of Library and Information Studies patterned after Project LOEX.

TENTH ANNUAL CONFERENCE
ON
LIBRARY ORIENTATION
FOR
ACADEMIC LIBRARIES

May 8 & 9, 1980

EASTERN MICHIGAN UNIVERSITY

REGISTRANTS

Jonette Aarstad
Reference Librarian
Clifford Library
University of Evansville
Evansville, IN 47702

Suzanne Aiardo
Ass't Librarian/State Documents
University Library
Suny at Albany
1400 Washington Ave.
Albany, NY 12222

Thomas V. Atkins
Chief, Instruction Services
Baruch College
CUNY
New York, NY 10010

Judith Avery
Instruction Librarian
Undergraduate Library
University of Michigan
Ann Arbor, MI 48109

Betsy Baker
Ass't Reference Librarian
University of Illinois
 at Urbana-Champaign
Urbana, IL 61801

Barbara Baruth
University of Wisconsin--Parkside
Kenosha, WI 53141

Anne K. Beaubien
Soc. Sc. Ref. Librarian/
 Bibl. Instructor
University of Michigan
Graduate Library
Ann Arbor, MI 48109

Teri L. Blasko
Reference Librarian
Eiche Library
Pennsylvania State Univ./
 Altoona Campus
Altoona, PA 16603

Deborah K. Blouin
Orientation/Instruction Coord.
University Library
Arizona State University
Tempe, AZ 85281

Harry Boonstra
Directory of Libraries
Van Zoeren Library
Hope College
Holland, MI 49423

151

Debbie Brown
Assistant Librarian
Firelands College Library
Bowling Green State University
Huron, OH 44839

Annette K. Buurstra
Education Librarian
Northeastern Illinois University
5500 N. St. Louis Ave.
Chicago, IL 60625

Joanne C. Callard
Interlibrary Loan Librarian
University of Oklahoma
Health Sciences Center Library
Oklahoma City, OK 73069

Virginia Cameron
Head, Special Materials Center
Drake Memorial Library
State University of New York/
  College at Brockport
Brockport, NY 14420

Susan M. Campbell
Science Librarian
Colgate University Library
Hamilton, NY 13346

Paul G. Cappuzzello
Instruction Librarian
University of Toledo Libraries
Toledo, OH 43606

Michele Cash
Reference Librarian
Lewis University
Route 53
Romeoville, IL 60441

Joan Chambers
Ass't Univ. Librarian for
  Public Services
Central University of CA,

San Diego
La Jolla, CA 92093

Beth Christensen
Music and Reference Librarian
Saint Olaf College
Northfield, MN 55057

Jeff Clark
Ass't Librarian -- Reference
Library/Media Center
SUNY College at Old Westbury
Old Westbury, NY 11568

Bonnie Collier
Reference Librarian
Sterling Memorial Library
Yale University Library
New Haven, CT 06477

Patrick Condon
Chief Librarian
Main Campus
Caulfield Institute of Technology
Caulfield East
Victoria, 3145, Australia

Martha H. Cordova
Head Reference Librarian
Colgate University Library
Hamilton, NY 13346

Lisa Cornelisse
Ass't Science Librarian
Science Library
Mass. Institute of Technology
Cambridge, MA 02139

Julie Czisny
Coordinator, Media Center
Golda Meir Library
Univ. of Wisconsin--Milwaukee
Milwaukee, WI 53201

Doris B. Dantin

Instructor
Dept. of Books and Libraries
Louisiana State University
Baton Rouge, LA 70803

Philip N. Dare
Reference Librarian
M.I. King Library
University of Kentucky
Lexington, KY 40506

Nancy M. Davidson
Ref. Lib.--Coordinator Bibl.
  Instruction
Dacus Library
Winthrop College
Rock Hill, SC 29733

Jeanne R. Dolgin
Head Instructional Librarian
Mercy College Library
Dobbs Ferry, NY 10522

Eileen Dubin
Interlibrary Loan
Northern Illinois Univ. Library
DeKalb, IL 60115

Gorman Duffett
Ass't Director Public Services
Cleveland State University
Cleveland, OH 44115

Russell Duino
Librarian/Bibliographer
Metropolitan Campus Library
Cuyahoga Community College
Cleveland, OH 44115

Rheba Dupras
Reference/Cataloger
Spahr Library
Dickinson College
Carlisle, PA 17013

Justin DuVall
Ass't Lib./Periodicals Lib.
St. Meinrad Archabbey Library
St. Meinrad College & School of
  Theology
St. Meinrad, IN 47577

Anita Evans
Ass't Head
Undergraduate Library
Michigan State Univ. Library
East Lansing, MI 48824

Nancy Fjällbrant
Duputy Librarian
Chalmers Institute of Technology
Gothenburg, Sweden

Dale G. Fleeger
Circulation Librarian
Wilson Library
Anderson College
Anderson, IN 46012

Elaine N. Flint
Librarian-Acquisitions
Instructional Materials Center
Glendale Community College
Glendale, AZ 85302

Virginia Frank
Reference/Bibliographic Inst.
Staley Library
Millikin University
Decatur, IL 62522

Roger W. Fromm
College Archivist/Ref. Lib.
Harvey A. Andruss Library
Bloomsburg State College
Bloomsburg, PA 17815

Alice H. Gadsden
Reference Librarian

Jackson Library
UNC--Greensboro
Greensboro, NC 27412

Mary W. George
Reference Librarian
Harlan Hatcher Grad. Library
University of Michigan
Ann Arbor, MI 48109

Sr. Mary Joan Gleason
Faculty Services Librarian
Lorette Wilmot Library
Nazareth College of Rochester
Rochester, NY 14610

Lillian Goldin
Coord. of Public Services
Library
North Shore Community College
Beverly, MA 01915

Kathy Graham
LOEX Secretary
Center of Educational Resrouces
Eastern Michigan University
Ypsilanti, MI 48197

Bonnie Gratch
Reference Librarian
Drake Memorial Library
State Univ. of NY at Brockport
Brockport, NY 14420

Phillip Greer
Ref./Instruction Librarian
Undergraduate Library
Indiana University
Bloomington, IN 47401

Susane Gruca
Library Science Intern
IPCD/Library Program
Central Michigan University
Troy, MI 48084

Larry Hardesty
Head, Ref. Dept. &
   CLR–NEH Project Director
Roy O. West Library
DePauw University
Greencastle, IN 46135

Richard Higginbotham
Instruction Librarian
Northeastern Illinois University
5500 N. St. Louis Ave.
Chicago, IL 60625

Sharon Hogan
Assistant to the Director
Harlan Hatcher Graduate Library
University of Michigan
Ann Arbor, MI 48109

Robert J. Hohl
Reference & Instruction Librarian
St. Mary's College Library
Notre Dame, IN 46556

Frances L. Hopkins
NEH/CLR Project Coordinator
Fackenthal Library
Franklin & Marshall College
Lancaster, PA 17604

Monroe Hopkins
Librarian
Dulany Library
William Woods College
Fulton, MO 65251

G. Lynn Hufford
Public Services Librarian
Gardner--Harvey Library
Miami University--Middletown
Middletown, OH 45042

Pauline Hunsberger
Reference Librarian
Walter E. Helmke Library

154

Indiana--Purdue at Fort Wayne
Fort Wayne, IN 46805

M. Huston--Miyamoto
Member of the Faculty
Library
The Evergreen State College
Olympia, WA 98505

Gerald J. Jacobson
Librarian
Dr. Martin Luther College
New Ulm, MN 56073

Lorraine A. Jean
Reference Librarian
General Education Library
Northern Illinois University
DeKalb, IL 60115

George T. Johnson
Library Director
Hallie Q. Brown Memorial
Central State University
Wilberforce, OH 45384

Thomas H. Kelly
Director, Library/Media
John Glenn High School
Wayne--Westland Schools
Wayne, MI 48184

Donald J. Kenney
Ass't General Ref. Library
Newman Library
Virginia Tech.
Blacksburg, VA 24061

Michael Keresztesi
Ass't Professor
School of Library Science
Wayne State University
Detroit, MI 48202

Bonnie Jean King

Business Subj. Sp.--Instr. Lib. Adm.
Carlson Library
University of Toledo
2801 W. Bancroft
Toledo, OH 43606

David N. King
Research Associate
Undergraduate Library
University of Illinois
Urbana, IL 61801

Thomas G. Kirk, Acting Director
Univ. of Wisconsin--Parkside
Kenosha, WI 53141

Carolyn Kirkendall
LOEX Director
Center of Educational Resources
Eastern Michigan University
Ypsilanti, MI 48197

Nancy M. Kline
Head, Lib. Orientation &
  Instr. Serv. Dept.
University of Connecticut Library
Storrs, CT 06268

Judy Koor
Library Instruction Librarian
Bracken Library
Ball State University
Muncie, IN 47304

John Kupersmith
Reference Librarian
Van Pelt Library
University of Pennsylvania
Philadelphia, PA 19104

Marcia T. Ladd
Ref./Bibliographic Instr.
Solomon R. Baker Library
Bentley College
Waltham, MA 02154

Wilma Lampman
Reference Librarian
Morris Library
Southern Illinois University
Carbondale, IL 62901

Kay Langston
Ass't Educ. & Soc. Sc. Librarian
Education & Soc. Sc. Library
University of Illinois
Urbana, IL 61801

Gail H. Lawrence
Reference Librarian
Main Library
Ohio State University
Columbus, OH 43214

Celeste Leonard
Assistant Librarian
Mathematics (216 Altgeld Hall)
University of Illinois
Champaign, IL 61820

George H. Libbey
Coordinator of Instruction
Paley Library
Temple University
Philadelphia, PA 19122

Heather M. Lloyd
Reference Librarian
Oklahoma State Univ. Library
Stillwater, OK 74078

Patricia E. Lowrey
Bibliographic Instructor
Torreyson Library
Univ. of Central Arkansas
Conway, AR 72032

John Lubans, Jr.
Assistant Librarian
Downtown College
University of Houston

Houston, TX 77002

Marilyn Lutzker
Head, Reader Services
John Jay College of Criminal
  Justice
New York, NY 10019

James Maguire
Head, Media Services
Library
Univ. of Wisconsin--Parkside
Kenosha, WI 53141

Edward D. Marman
Director, Library/Media
Marshall Junior High School
Wayne--Westland Schools
Wayne, MI 48184

Laurel S. Maughan
Bibliographic Instr. Coordinator
William Jasper Kerr Library
Oregon State University
Corvallis, OR 97330

Patrick Max
Coord. of Library Instruction
Univ. of Notre Dame
Memorial Library
Notre Dame, IN 46556

Gerry Meek
Orientation Librarian
The Library
University of Waterloo
Waterloo, Ontario, Canada

Constance Mellon
Coord. of Bibl. Instruction
Univ. of Tennessee at
  Chattanooga
Chattanooga, TN 37401

Wayne Meyer

Periodicals Ref. Librarian
Bracken Library
Ball State University
Muncie, IN 47304

M. Ann Miller
Reference Librarian
College of the Mainland
Texas City, TX 77590

Ruth Miller
Acquisitions/Ref. Librarian
Clifford Library
University of Evansville
Evansville, IN 47702

Mary F. Minock
Reference Librarian
Arts and Sciences
Lansing Community College
Lansing, MI 48901

Joan M. Mitchell
Ref. & Media Serv. Librarian
Butler County Comm. College
Library
Butler, PA 16001

Thomas J. Moore
Library Instruction Coordinator
Bracken Library
Ball State University
Muncie, IN 47306

Esther Nelson
Assistant Professor
Western Illinois Univ. Library
Macomb, IL 61455

Steven Cameron Newsome
Ass't Reference Librarian
University Library
Univ. of Illinois at Chicago Circle
Chicago, IL 60680

Cerise Oberman-Soroka
Head, Reference
College of Charleston Library
Charleston, SC 29401

Molly O'Hara
Ass't Reference Librarian
Univ. of Chicago at Chicago Circle
Chicago, IL 60680

Jerilyn K. Oltman
Instructional Services Librarian
Carl Sandburg College Library
Galesburg, IL 61401

Patricia Ormiston
Social Science Librarian
Miami University Library
Oxford, OH 45056

Dick Pantano
Library Director
Shapiro Library
New Hampshire College
Manchester, NH 03104

Maureen Pastine
Reference Librarian
University Library
Univ. of IL at Urbana--Champaign
Urbana, IL 61801

Penny Pearson
Head, Undergraduate Library
Ohio State University
Columbus, OH 43201

Vi Perlmutter
Reference Librarian
Learning Resources Center
Thomas More College
Ft. Mitchell, KY 41017

Billie Peterson

Reference Librarian
West Campus LRC
Ohio State University
Columbus, OH 43210

Kathy Phillips
Circulation Librarian
Learning Resources Center
Thomas More College
Ft. Mitchell, KY 41017

Penelope Pillsbury
Reference Librarian
Bailey--Howe Library
University of Vermont
Burlington, VT 05405

Marcia P. Preston
Assistant Librarian
Univ. of Mich.--Dearborn Library
Dearborn, MI 48128

Judith Pryor
Univ. of Wisconsin--Parkside
Kenosha, WI 53141

Hannelore B. Rader
Coord. Ed./Psych. Division
Center of Educational Resources
Eastern Michigan University
Ypsilanti, MI 48917

Mary Reichel
Senior Reference Librarian
Undergraduate Library
SUNY at Buffalo
Amherst, NY 14260

Rosemary Rice--Billings
Reference Librarian
Saginaw Valley State College
Library
2250 Pierce Road
University Center, MI 48710

Sharon J. Rogers
Coordinator, Library Programs
Carlson Library
University of Toledo
Toledo, OH 43606

Lynne Ruben
Assistant Professor
Western Illinois Univ. Library
Macomb, IL 61455

Tim Schobert
Orientation Librarian
Morisset Library
University of Ottawa
Ottawa, Ontario, Canada
K1N 9A5

Wesley Schram
Library Instruction Coordinator
G. Flint Purdy Library
Wayne State University
Detroit, MI 48203

Barbara Schwartz
Coordinator, Instructional Prog.
Undergraduate Library
Univ. of Texas at Austin
Austin, TX 78712

Diane G. Schwartz
Associate Librarian
Medical Center Library
University of Michigan
Ann Arbor, MI 48109

Karen S. Seibert
Head of Reference
Main Library, Box 8198
Univ. of IL at Chicago Circle
Chicago, IL 60680

Rose Marie Service
Education--Psychology Librarian

University of Oregon Library
Eugene, OR 97403

Dr. Y.S. Sim
Reference Librarian
Mercer County College Library
P.O. Box B
Trenton, NJ 08690

Fred Smith
Librarian
McGill Library
Westminster College
New Wilmington, PA 16142

Fred E. Smith
Coordinator Library Instruction
Ezra Lehman Library
Shippensburg State College
Shippensburg, PA 17257

Mary Kay Smith
Instructional Services Librarian
A.C. Clark Library
Bemidji State University
Bemidji, MN 56601

Marvin Southworth
Director
Grady C. Hogue LRC
Bee County College
Beeville, TX 78102

Molly Spinney
Reference Librarian
McGill Library
Westminster College
New Wilmington, PA 16142

Peter Spyers--Duran
Directory of Univ. Library
California State Univ.--Long Beach
Long Beach, CA 90840

Keith Stanger

Orientation Librarian
Center of Educational Resources
Eastern Michigan University
Ypsilanti, MI 48197

Susan Swords Steffen
Reader's Services Librarian
Byrne Memorial Library
St. Xavier College
103d and Central Park
Chicago, IL 60655

Laurie St. Laurent
Library Instructor
Transylvania University Library
Transylvania University
Lexington, KY 40508

Carla J. Stoffle
Assistant Vice--Chancellor
Univ. of Wisconsin--Parkside
Kenosha, WI 53141

Richard Swain
Ref. Lib. -- Humanities
Cleveland State University
Cleveland, OH 44115

Roger Sween
Reference Librarian
Learning Resources
St. Cloud State University
St. Cloud, MN 56301

Susan Marie Szasz
Ass't Reference Librarian
Uris Undergraduate Library
Cornell University
Ithaca, NY 14853

Kal Szekely
Bowling Green State University
Bowling Green, OH 43402

Auda V. Taylor

Reference Librarian
Holland (Soc. Sc. & Hum.)
Library
Washington State University
Pullman, WA 99163

Virginia Tiefel
Director
Library User Education
OSU Libraries
Ohio State University
Columbus, OH 43210

Gregory M. Toth
Bibl. Instr./Humanities Librarian
Wallace Memorial Library
Rochester Institute of Technology
Rochester, NY 14623

Shannon M. Troy
Ref. Lib. & Coord. Lib. User Ed.
Governors State University
Park Forest So., IL 60466

Michael VanHouten
Reference Librarian
Shipman Library
Adrian College
Adrian, MI 49221

Judith Violette
Head, Ref. Department
Helmke Library
Indiana Univ.--Purdue Univ.
 at Ft. Wayne
Fort Wayne, IN 46805

Kathleen Voight
University of Toledo Library
Toledo, OH 43606

Deborah Walsh
Reference Librarian
Rosary College Library
River Forest, IL 60305

James E. Ward
Directory of the Library
Crisman Memorial Library
David Lipscomb College
Nashville, TN 37203

James A. Warrington, Jr.
Science Librarian
Wildman Science Library
Earlham College
Richmond, IN 47374

Patricia Wathen
Reader's Service Librarian
Sarah Lawrence College Library
21 Village Lane
Bronxville, NY 10108

Laura Whayne
Assistant Librarian
Wallerstedt Library
Bethany College
Lindsborg, KS 67456

Dixie Whittington
Assoc. Prof./Reference Librarian
Watson Library
Northwestern State University
Natchitoches, LA 71457

Calvin Williams
Head, Reference Department
Saginaw Valley State College
Library
2250 Pierce Road
University Center, MI 48170

Sandra Yee
Coordinator, Library Services
Muskegon Community College
Muskegon, MI 49442

160